PRAISE FOR

Bonhoeffer and Business Ethics

Walt Padelford is to be applauded for this work on BONHOEFFER AND BUSINESS ETHICS, which not only provides fresh perspective on the challenging work of Dietrich Bonhoeffer, but offers insightful application for the field of business ethics.

I can envision this volume making a significant difference in business classes for both professors and students in days ahead. Moreover, this fine book will certainly have a powerful influence for all who seek to live as faithful followers of Jesus Christ.

—David S. Dockery
President, Union University

BONHOEFFER AND BUSINESS ETHICS raises the bar. Dr. Padelford escorts us through the maturing of Dietrich Bonhoeffer as he journeyed from pacifism to being a participant in the plot to kill Hitler. The lesson: life in the world is the crucible where Christ is manifested, and this is life's highest objective–also for business ethics. Christ takes form in the world of business through the inner struggles of those in whom He lives as they engage in the rough and tumble of the marketplace. Ethical principles, ideas, and formulations are the milk of the classroom but poor substitutes for the real challenges encountered in the fallen world. The centrality of Christ; an understanding of the stresses faced in commerce; and the spiritual formation of the lives of students: these three essentials should be tackled in Christian Business Schools.

The book is a "wonderful read" for anybody interested in business, business ethics, or practical theology.

—Richard Chewning
Emeritus Professor of Christian Ethics
Baylor University

PRAISE FOR

Bonhoeffer and Business Ethics

In an era in which our society thinks that business has lost its moral compass, we wonder who has been teaching our financial leaders ethics. When conventional approaches to morality fail, we are driven to look for models of how to live godly lives in an age averse to righteousness. Few figures in history inspire us in this way better than Dietrich Bonhoeffer.

In his new book, Walton Padelford has done a great service to both the church and financial sector. He has shown the implications of Bonhoeffer's moral courage to business ethics. This is a creative, challenging, and needful project for our times.

—Greg A. Thornbury
Dean, School of Theology and Missions
Union University

Because of the failures in the business world today there is an increasing need to teach business ethics in our University business schools. Many business schools are realizing this and are exploring ways to meet this need. Dr. Walt Padelford has done a masterful job of writing a book on ethics that covers it from many perspectives.

I believe this will be a great tool for any business school to use.

—Harry L. Smith
former Chairman and CEO of Schilling Enterprises
Author of *Driven to Deliver*
Executive in Residence,
University of Memphis-
Fogelman School of Business and Economics

BONHOEFFER

AND BUSINESS ETHICS

PADELFORD

BONHOEFFER

AND

BUSINESS ETHICS

BY

WALTON PADELFORD

UNION UNIVERSITY

BORDERSTONE PRESS, LLC

2011

First American Edition

BORDERSTONE PRESS, LLC

Bonhoeffer and Business Ethics

Author: Walton Padelford
Cover Design: Kirby Atkins
Cover Author Portrait: Jim Veneman - Union University
Interior Design: BorderStone Press, LLC

© 2011 BorderStone Press, LLC

Copy editor: Roger Duke
Supervising editor: Brian R. Mooney

Published by BorderStone Press, LLC, PO Box 1383, Mountain Home, AR 72654
Memphis, TN - Dallas, TX

www.borderstonepress.com

ISBN: 978-1-936670-14-7

Library of Congress Control Number: 2011911700

CONTENTS

Preface

Chapter 1 - HIS COSTLY DISCIPLESHIP 1

Chapter 2 - ETHICS 31

Fundamental Problem of Business Ethics 33

Adam Smith & Modern Economic Thought 36

Our Present Condition 39

The Four Mandates 43

Government 46

Marriage and Labor as Divine Institutions 50

God's Commandments and Business Ethics 52

Chapter 3 - DISCOURSE ON BUSINESS ETHICS 57

Personal Formation as Business Ethics 65

Business Ethics as Formation 67

The Church and Formation 70

The Church and Business 78

Chapter 4 - BEYOND BENTHAM AND KANT 85

Bentham 87

Kant 90

Beyond Bentham and Kant 94

Individual or Social Ethics 102

Chapter 5 - BUSINESS AS A MANDATE OF GOD 107

Business as Preparing the Way 112

Business as Part of the Natural World 115

Businesspersons and Institutions 119

Chapter 6 - COMMERCE AND THE GLORY OF GOD . 127

Chapter 7 - BUSINESS AS THE VOID 139

Business as a Penultimate Pursuit 146

The Success Syndrome 150

The Idolization of Success 154

Failure in Business 157

The view from below 160

Chapter 8 - VOCATION 163

Responsible Business Life 170

Rejection of All Secular New Men 178

The Businessperson as Disciple 180

Personal Reflection 188

Chapter 9 - AUTHORITY AND POWER 191

Chapter 10 - BONHOEFFER'S CONSISTENT ETHICAL
RESPONSE: *From Pacifist to Conspirator* 201

Pastor Bonhoeffer 209

The Borderline Case 213

Epilogue - CHRISTIAN FORMATION IN THE BUSINESS SCHOOL .. 219

About the Author

PREFACE

THE AVAILABILITY of the *Dietrich Bonhoeffer Works*, English edition, provides an entrance into much more of the Bonhoeffer corpus for English-speaking readers. This massive translation work has been undertaken under the auspices of The International Bonhoeffer Society, English language section. Translation is being done from the *Dietrich Bonhoeffer Werke*, the expertly edited and definitive edition of Bonhoeffer's works in German. Fortress Press is publishing these works as soon as they are made available.

In some of the footnotes in which a book is mentioned for the first time, I have used the initials DBWE for Dietrich Bonhoeffer Works, English edition. These English volumes of previously unattainable Bonhoeffer material have made the research for this book possible. I have used some other editions of Bonhoeffer's books as well. In the case of *Ethics*, I have used a previous edition as well as the Fortress Press edition. Quotations from the Bible other than Bonhoeffer's quotes have been taken from The Reformation Study Bible, English Standard Version, noted in the references.

This book has several purposes. I wanted to try to say something distinctively Christian about the whole topic of business ethics. As I mention in the text, I have been disappointed by my own performance in teaching. I am not sure that a distinctively Christian point of view has been manifested to the students. Of course, the next question is, "What is the distinctively Christian point of view with respect to business ethics?" I have tried to broach this question using as my main framework Bonhoeffer's book, *Ethics*.

The second purpose is to introduce a new generation of college students to the works of Dietrich Bonhoeffer. I find them to be always edifying, always uplifting. I hope the new generation will find them that way also. Bonhoeffer's four classics are *The Cost of Discipleship* [now simply *Discipleship* from Fortress Press], *Life Together*, *Ethics*, and *Letters and Papers from Prison*. I find that there is continuing interest in him—in his work and in his amazing life story. The definitive biography of Bonhoeffer is by his great friend, Eberhard Bethge, entitled *Dietrich Bonhoeffer, A Biography*. I have also used this resource freely in writing this book. I hope that many will begin to read and re-read these classics.

The third purpose is to use some of the themes in Bonhoeffer to think in a challenging way about business and the opportunities for real discipleship in business—might we say for real sanctification in business? This may be something new, and I hope that it will provoke reflection and discussion.

I would like to thank my assistant, Landon Preston who has helped me with research and reading and editing manuscript. I thank my wife, Katy, for being patient and loving while, for the last year, I have hidden away in my study to read and write.

—Walton Padelford
Union University

CHAPTER 1

HIS COSTLY DISCIPLESHIP

DIETRICH BONHOEFFER was the sixth child born to Dr. Karl Bonhoeffer and Paula von Hase. There would eventually be eight children in that academic, well-cultured family. Dr. Bonhoeffer, head of a clinic in Breslau at the time of Dietrich's birth on February 4, 1906, would eventually move to Berlin where he would occupy the chair of psychiatry and neurology at the University of Berlin. He was also director of the Berlin Charité clinic. Dietrich's mother, Paula, was from an aristocratic family. Her father was a professor of theology and court preacher to Kaiser Wilhelm II. In such a family atmosphere the children absorbed great literary works read aloud by their father. Their mother taught them at home during the first years of school, and contributed to their liveliness of mind. The Bonhoeffer's home was open to visitors and guests; aunts, uncles, cousins, students and friends would visit and stay for a few days. It is clear that Dietrich was brought up in one of the elite families in Germany—patriotic, not extravagantly nationalistic, responsible, humanistic, and university-oriented.

The Bonhoeffer's idyllic world was shattered with the onset of World War I and the death of their oldest son, Walter, in an advance by the German troops in 1918. Dietrich received Walter's confirmation Bible at his own confirmation, and used it throughout his life for personal meditation and worship.[1]

The Bonhoeffers were not a church-going family. Karl Bonhoeffer stated that he never understood religion. Religious instruction fell to Paula who read Bible stories to the children out of an illustrated Bible. Dietrich continued Bible reading at night as a lad. His governess, Käthe Horn, from the Herrnhut community (Moravian Brethren) certainly did not forbid this.[2] In Dietrich's last year of high school as the class was responding to the teacher's question as to what they wanted to do in life, Dietrich declared his desire to study theology. His father and brothers tried to dissuade him, but with no success. So at the age of seventeen in 1924, Dietrich matriculated at the University of Tübingen where he spent two semesters. He studied with Adolf Schlatter and Karl Heim. From Schlatter he received a sense of the authority of Scripture. Indeed, belief in the authority of the Scriptures would help Bonhoeffer later to understand Karl Barth, one of the most influential

---

[1] Eberhard Bethge, *Dietrich Bonhoeffer: A Biography* (Minneapolis, MN: Fortress Press, 2000), 28.

[2] F. Burton Nelson, "The Life of Dietrich Bonhoeffer," *The Cambridge Companion to Dietrich Bonhoeffer*, ed. John W. de Gruchy (Cambridge: Cambridge University Press, 2002), 27.

theologians of the twentieth century, so well. Karl Heim taught systematic theology, in which he aimed at unity of knowledge rather than the modern dichotomy between faith and reason.[3]

Dietrich then registered at Berlin University, where he studied under such eminent German theologians as Karl Holl, Reinhold Seeberg, and Adolf von Harnack. The Harnacks lived near the Bonhoeffers in Berlin. The families knew each other well. Dietrich attended three semesters of seminar classes on church history taught by Harnack. Under Holl, Dietrich spent much time learning the theology of Martin Luther, and under Seeberg, the systematic theologian, he wrote his dissertation, *Sanctorum Communio*, completed in 1927 at the incredibly young age of twenty-one. The dissertation was a theological-sociological study of the church with the predominant theme of "Christ existing as church-community." Karl Barth described it as a theological miracle. During his student days in Berlin, Dietrich had good success leading a Sunday School class and a youth group. After this, he went to Barcelona as a probationary minister with a German-speaking congregation.

Upon his return to Berlin he began work on his *Habilitationsschrift*, or qualifying thesis, for a post as lecturer. The title of this work is *Act and Being*. Bonhoeffer described it in a letter to his professor, Seeberg. "It connects to the question of consciousness and conscience in theology

---

[3] Martin Rumscheidt, "The Formation of Bonhoeffer's Theology," *The Cambridge Companion to Dietrich Bonhoeffer* (Cambridge: Cambridge University Press, 2002), 52-53.

and to several Luther citations from the major Galatians commentary."[4] Dietrich gave his inaugural lecture at Berlin on July 31, 1930, "The Question of Man in Contemporary Philosophy and Theology." At that time, at Berlin, he was the youngest assistant lecturer at the age of twenty-four. After a year he received a grant for post-doctoral study at Union Theological Seminary in New York.

While at Union, Dietrich became good friends with Paul and Marion Lehman, Franklin Fisher, and Paul Lasserre. The Lehmans became his close American friends. He enjoyed fellowship in their home on many occasions. Through Franklin Fisher, an African-American seminarian, he gained access to the Abyssinian Baptist Church in Harlem, where he taught children's classes and participated in the Sunday services on a regular basis. It was here, Bonhoeffer said, "I heard the gospel preached....Here one really could still hear someone talk in a Christian sense about sin and grace and the love of God and ultimate hope."[5] Paul Lasserre was a pacifist and wanted "to be a saint." He made Dietrich aware of the radical demands of the Sermon on the Mount so that in writing to his brothers he said: "I think I know that I would really become clear and honest with myself if I really began to take the Sermon on the Mount seriously....There are things which it is worth supporting without compromise. And it seems to me that

---

[4] Dietrich Bonhoeffer, *Act and Being*, DBWE, Vol. 2 (Minneapolis: Fortress Press, 1996), 3.
[5] Dietrich Bonhoeffer, *Barcelona, Berlin, New York 1928-1931*, DBWE Vol. 10 (Minneapolis: Fortress Press, 2008), 30.

these include peace and social justice, or in fact Christ."[6] These individuals were part of Dietrich's theological development also.

In June, 1931, he returned to Berlin from America. He didn't stay at his parent's home long, for he was off to Bonn on July 10, to meet with Karl Barth whose theology he had been reading for some time. Barth's theology has been called dialectical theology. He stressed the fact that God is transcendent, the "wholly other", so that He cannot be characterized with a simple formula. Bonhoeffer's theology has some of this characteristic also. Statements about God must perhaps be paradoxical, with each affirmation balanced by a negation to do justice to God's infinite transcendence. It was in Bonn in one of Barth's evening discussion groups that Bonhoeffer added a comment from Luther to the discussion. "The curses of the godless sometimes sound better to God's ear than the hallelujahs of the pious." This comment delighted Barth.[7]

Bonhoeffer worked as assistant lecturer in systematic theology at the University of Berlin, where theological studies were booming. More than one thousand students were studying theology there. Commenting on the summer term lecture on "The Nature of the Church," Wolf-Dieter Zimmerman stated, "In the lecture room Bonhoeffer was very concentrated, quite unsentimental, almost dispassionate, clear as crystal, with a certain rational coldness, like a reporter." One day after arriving twenty

---

[6] Renate Wind, *Dietrich Bonhoeffer: A Spoke in the Wheel* (Grand Rapids, MI: Wm. B. Eerdmans Publishing Co., 1998), 53-54.

[7] Bethge, 175.

minutes late for class, Professor Bonhoeffer said, "One of my boys is dying, and I wanted to have a last word with him."[8] Bonhoeffer's "boys" were a confirmation class from the working-class suburb of Wedding, to which he had been appointed by his church authorities.

The confirmands at Wedding were totally boisterous and out of control when Bonhoeffer arrived. He began by telling them of some of his experiences in Harlem. That got their attention. He took an apartment in their district in order to devote himself more fully to these youngsters. A sort of "community-club" was formed out of this group where young people from the streets and surrounding neighborhood could gather, discuss issues, play chess, and take weekend trips, as well as hear stories from America and stories from the Bible. This was an early experiment with "religionless Christianity" and "Life Together," which were themes throughout Bonhoeffer's entire life and work.[9]

Dietrich was ordained to the gospel ministry on November 15, 1931, in the Matthew Church near Potsdam Place. He spent 1931 and 1932 in much ecumenical activity with the World Alliance. He was always encouraging the development of an adequate theological basis for the ecumenical movement, and the forthrightness to deliver a message of peace as the commandment of God. The theme of peace was the major focus of his early ecumenical work. There was no need for the Church to justify a commandment of God; simply deliver it.

---

[8] Wolf-Dieter Zimmermann, "Years in Berlin," *I Knew Dietrich Bonhoeffer*, ed. Wolf-Dieter Zimmermann (New York: Harper & Row, 1966), 62, 66.

[9] Bethge, 226-227.

6

On February 1, 1933, two days after Hitler's accession to power on January 30, the young lecturer gave a radio broadcast entitled, "The Leader and the Individual in the Younger Generation." The invitation was probably worked out through the university. The lecture was cut off and not allowed to be completed. It is amazing how early Bonhoeffer saw the way things were going with the Fuhrer, particularly as most of the Protestant church was joyfully falling in line behind Hitler. Already in existence was a Protestant group which called itself "The German Christians." Its aim was to combine Christianity with National Socialism. Hitler reciprocated this good feeling by ordering whole SA units to attend church. How quickly the party's true colors showed. "By 1934 party leaders were discouraging church membership in the SA;..."[10]

In June-July 1933, the lines in the church struggle were more clearly revealed through the appointment of August Jäger as president of the high church council through devious political maneuvering. Bonhoeffer, and his good friend Franz Hildebrandt, became more radicalized by calling for a pastor's strike, i.e., a refusal to perform funerals. The ministers did not agree with this proposal. Nevertheless, for upcoming church elections in July, Dietrich worked hard for candidates of the Young Reformation movement. The campaigning was made more difficult by intimidation from Hitler's SA troops. As a result, the pro-National Socialist candidates received over seventy percent of the vote. After this defeat Bonhoeffer preached on July 23; "...come...all of

---

[10] Dietrich Bonhoeffer, *London, 1933-1935*, DBWE Vol. 13 (Minneapolis: Fortress Press, 2007), 44.

you who are abandoned and left alone, we will go back to the Holy Scriptures, we will go and look for the church together....Let the church remain the church...confess, confess, confess!"[11] This sermon was an indication that perhaps the church might have to enter into a *status confessionis* based on a clear statement of faith in Christ and a clear statement as to what a church should preach and do. This is a serious step declaring a state of confessional protest against an ecclesiastical entity which has become heterodox, such an entity being in violation of Scripture and the creeds (Apostle's, Nicene).

In July the Young Reformation movement decided to write such a confession. They appointed Bonhoeffer and two other young theologians to work on it. They were to travel to the Bethel community during the month of August to work. The Bethel community located in Westphalia had facilities for the care of the disabled as well as a theological college. The Bethel confession made explicit the doctrine of the Trinity and the Person of Christ. It also dealt clearly and negatively with the Aryan clause of the civil service law. The Aryan clause prohibited anyone of Jewish descent from serving in the German civil service. This affected the churches because ministers were on the payroll of the state and hence members of the German civil service. This clause, if adopted by the church, would make it impossible for Christians of Jewish background to train for the Christian ministry.

The Bethel Confession was coolly received by the church at large. In the infamous "Brown Synod" (so-called because

---

[11] Bonhoeffer, *London*, 296.

of the sea of Hitler's brown shirted para-military troops in attendance) the Aryan paragraph was adopted by the national church. Bonhoeffer had made up his mind that he must withdraw from the national church in this event. This was also the end of ministry in the national church for Franz Hildebrandt and Bonhoeffer's brother-in-law Gerhard Leibholz, both of Jewish descent. At this point two thousand pastors signed a resolution to reverse the Aryan clause; among them was Pastor Martin Niemöller, a former U-boat commander in World War I.

Pastor Niemöller founded the Pastor's Emergency League to protest inclusion of the Aryan paragraph in the order of the national church. This was a step toward the formation of the Confessing Church. On September 12, 1933, Pastor Niemöller called on German pastors to commit to the following four points: "(1) To a new allegiance to the Scriptures and confessions, (2) to resist infringement of these, (3) to give financial help to those affected by the law or by violence, and (4) to reject the Aryan clause."[12] By the end of 1933 the Pastors' Emergency League had six thousand members. At this time an offer came to Dietrich to assume the pastorates of two German-speaking congregations in London, one in Sydenham, the other in the East End. He accepted this new situation and moved to London. He was aided in this work by Franz Hildebrandt. Dietrich felt that his effectiveness was at a low ebb in the church struggle, and he needed time to sort things out.

While in London Dietrich became good friends with George Bell, the Bishop of Chichester, and a leader in the

---

[12] Bonhoeffer, *London*, 309.

ecumenical movement. Bonhoeffer continued to inform Bell
and the ecumenical movement of the situation in the
churches in Germany, and to impress upon them the need to
support the newly forming Confessing Movement, which
was growing in its opposition to the national church. By
December of 1933 the youth organizations of the national
church had been handed over to the Hitler Youth
movement, the *Hitler Jungen*, by Reich Bishop Müller,[13] the
president of the high church council of the Old Prussian
Union which was a major component of the German
National Church. The opposition churches became known
as the Confessing Church. They had entered into *status
confessionis*.

On May 29 – 31, 1934, opposition churches met in
Barmen and agreed upon the famous Barmen declaration
which had been written by Karl Barth. In it the Confessing
churches made an evangelical confession of faith and
opposed the false doctrine of the German Christians by
rejecting: "...the false teaching that the church can and must
recognize other events, powers, images and truths as divine
revelation alongside the one word of God, as a source of its
preaching..."[14] The Confessing Church was formed as a
result of the Barmen Synod and the Dahlem Synod. Dahlem
was a Berlin suburb where the Confessing churches met in
October, 1934, to establish an emergency church
government against the Reich church government. It was
called the Council of Brethren of the German Evangelical
Church. The church struggle in Germany thus entered a

---

[13] Wind, 82.
[14] Ibid., 371.

new era. Following Barmen and the Synod of Dahlem, the Confessing Churches rejected the authority of the Reich Church and the authority of Reich Bishop Ludwig Müller.

The previous March the Reich Bishop had ordered the seminaries of the Old Prussian Union to be closed. The Confessing Church, therefore, undertook to open its own seminaries. There were eventually five of these institutions. In preparing to train its own young pastors, the young firebrand in London was remembered as the best choice to lead in seminary training. Bonhoeffer was appointed to this post on January, 1935, with an agreement to begin his duties in March of that year.

In August, 1934, Dietrich had taken part in the ecumenical youth conference at Fanö, Denmark. It was here that he preached his famous peace sermon using as his text Psalm 85:8, "Let me hear what God the Lord will speak, for he will speak peace to his people, to his saints;..."

How does peace come about? Through a system of political treaties? Through the investment of international capital in different countries? Or through universal peaceful rearmament in order to guarantee peace? Through none of these, for the sole reason that in all of them peace is confused with safety. There is no way to peace along the way of safety....Once again how will peace come? Who will call us to peace so that the world will hear, will have to hear?... Only the one great ecumenical council of the holy church of Christ over all the world can speak out so that the world, though it gnash its teeth, will have to hear, so that the peoples will rejoice because the church of Christ in the name of Christ has taken the weapons from the hands of their sons, forbidden war, proclaimed the peace of Christ against the raging world."[15]

Bonhoeffer preached that Christians may not use weapons against each other because that would be using weapons against Christ himself. He, no doubt, saw the clouds of war gathering. Preaching peace was also connected with the freedom to proclaim the gospel and confess the faith in Germany, for he also foresaw   the terrible persecution time coming under Hitler. In other words, pacifism was a means of beginning to resist the Nazi regime.

In the Fall of 1934, Dietrich became intensely interested in visiting Mohandas Gandhi in India. He wanted to share in his daily life and learn the non-violent methods of resistance that Gandhi was using so successfully against the English colonial power. It is clear here that Bonhoeffer was not only resisting a Nazi heresy in the church, but he was resisting Nazism itself. He was resisting through the force of ideas (pacifism) and doing apprenticeship for political resistance through his desire to study with Gandhi. He was beginning to live out step by step his belief as to the proper relationship of the church to the state. In April, 1933, he had given a sermon to a group of Berlin pastors in which he outlined the church's degrees of response to a state which disregards basic human rights. First, the church may ask the state if its actions are legitimate *qua* state. Second, the church must aid the victims of wrongful state action even if these victims do not belong to the Christian community. Third, the church should not only bandage the victims

---

[15] Eberhard Bethge, Renate Bethge, and Christian Gremmels, *Dietrich Bonhoeffer: A Life in Pictures* (London: SCM Press, 1986), 133.

12

under the wheel, but put a spoke in the wheel itself. [16]
During his remaining days in London, Dietrich began work
on his classic exposition of the Sermon on the Mount, *The
Cost of Discipleship*. Although his plan to visit Gandhi did
not materialize, Dietrich did visit English seminaries and
religious communities in order to learn more about doing
the faith in community.

In April, 1935, Dietrich began his duties as seminary
instructor. To live together and learn and practice the
Sermon on the Mount became the *modus operandi* of this
seminary of the Confessing Church first located at Zingst in
the Rhineland Bible School on the Baltic Sea. Two months
later, the seminary moved to rooms in a former private
school at Finkenwalde near Stettin. This seminary was
financed by the voluntary gifts of church members of
Confessing churches. While at Finkenwalde, Bonhoeffer met
several families of the landed aristocracy with whom he
developed good friendships. One of his good friends was
Ruth von Kleist-Retzow, who took an interest in the
progress of his book, *Discipleship*, and also in the writings of
Karl Barth. Here Dietrich also met Maria von Wedemeyer,
Ruth's granddaughter, who eventually became his fiancée.

Twenty-three young pastors-in-training attended the first
semester of instruction by Dr. Bonhoeffer, including his
future great friend and biographer, Eberhard Bethge. Soon
the state would declare these seminaries to be illegal,
however, they continued on a more-or-less underground
basis; and for two and a half years, they did some great,
practical theological work.

---

[16] Wind, 69.

Meditation and prayer time were made part of the seminary rule. Living at close quarters showed the need to live as disciples of Christ. In the summer of 1935, Hitler attempted a rapprochement with the churches and removed some of the more radical German Christians (including Reich Bishop Müller) from power. Church committees were formed with invitations to members of the Confessing Church to participate. Those holding out for doctrinal purity within the larger national church were called the Confessing Movement. Those who would not join the national church again were called the Confessing Front. Clearly, Bonhoeffer was in the latter group, as well as many churches from the Old Prussian Union.

At this time, Karl Barth was expelled from Germany for his refusal to take the civil service loyalty oath containing the "Aryan clause." Both Barth and Bonhoeffer continued to be troubled by the failure of the Confessing Church to speak out clearly on the Jewish question. On December 2, 1935, the "fifth Decree" was enacted, which truly made ecclesiastical organizations outside the Reich church illegal; this included the seminary at Finkenwalde. Dietrich gave the seminarians the opportunity to leave. If even one wanted to stay, Dietrich assured them that he would stay as well. All twenty-three stayed. However, periodically, a student would go to the official church committee to be examined for the gospel ministry. When approved, he would be eligible for appointment and salary. For those not taking the official route, life could be hard and the future uncertain.

After the first term's work at Finkenwalde, Bonhoeffer sent a proposal to the Council of Brethren of the Old

Prussian Union for the purpose of gaining permission for a small group of students to remain at the seminary to help him with the work. These brothers, along with Bonhoeffer, would live a communal life in service to Christ and each other, and would aid the district churches in preaching and teaching, as well as helping with the next group of students. This community would be called the Evangelical House of Brethren. This experiment in community-living, work, meditation, and prayer lasted for two years, and resulted in the publication of a small volume by Dietrich, *Life Together*.[17]

On January 2 of the following year, the Finkenwalde community held a church service for the surrounding neighborhood. Dietrich preached a powerful sermon from Ezra 4 on the rebuilding of the wall around Jerusalem and the rejection of help from the opposition by Ezra and Nehemiah. The point was obvious. The church must resist interference by the state in church affairs. Only the Holy Spirit could help in renewing and rebuilding the church. In the afternoon the neighborhood congregation constituted itself as a Confessing congregation at Finkenwalde. They continued meeting well after the seminary had been closed.[18]

Through God's great provision, Bonhoeffer and all his seminarians were able to make a visit to fellow-believers in Sweden in 1936. This irritated the new Reich Bishop, Heckel, and further political maneuvering between him and the seminary ensued. This conflict resulted in the revocation

---

[17] Bethge, 466.
[18] Ibid., 501-502.

of Bonhoeffer's right to teach at the University of Berlin. The reasons given were two: Bonhoeffer's continued direction of the illegal seminary, and the seminary's visit to Sweden without permission from the Ministry of Education.[19]

A series of five retreats were held for former Finkenwalde students from 1936 until 1938. The first of these dealt with many current church questions, including "What is the church? When should fellowship be broken? When is church authority legitimate?"

This lecture on church-community was published in June, 1936. It was this lecture that contained the provocative phrase; "Whoever knowingly separates himself from the Confessing Church in Germany separates himself from salvation."[20] This statement made the rounds in hundreds of churches. Taken in the context of the whole lecture, some Confessing Churches supported Bonhoeffer's statement; some did not. This simply added to the atmosphere of debate and uncertainty.

In the Spring of 1936 the leadership of the Confessing Church prepared a memorandum to Hitler asking such questions as: "Was the de-Christianization of the people official government policy?" and "The new ideology was imposing an anti-Semitism that necessarily committed people to a hatred of the Jews, which parents had to combat in the education of their children."[21] This action paralleled Bonhoeffer's first principle of responsible church action if

---

[19] Ibid., 516.
[20] Ibid., 520.
[21] Ibid., 532.

the state dissolves basic human rights. The church may ask the state if its actions are legitimate state actions. Hitler made no response. However, the memorandum was copied and published abroad, thus placing the Confessing Church in a more dubious position vis-à-vis the German state. On August 23, the memorandum was read from many pulpits by Confessing pastors, whose names were noted by the Gestapo. The document was made public by Ernst Tillich, one of Bonhoeffer's pupils. Tillich, Werner Koch (another of Bonhoeffer's students) and Friedrich Weissler, the author of the memorandum, were arrested and sent to Sachsenhausen concentration camp. Weissler was immediately separated from the others because of his Jewish ancestry and died within a week—the first martyr of the Confessing Movement.

Bonhoeffer's *Discipleship* (originally published as *Cost of Discipleship* in English) was completed shortly before the closure of the seminary by the Gestapo in September, 1937. The closure occurred after increasing intimidation of Confessing pastors by the state. More regulations had been enacted, such as the forbidding of any church meetings on non-church property, forbidding the taking of collections, and reading names of arrested brethren publicly. Many in the Confessing church stood stoutly against this; therefore, there was an increasing wave of arrests and intimidation. Pastor Martin Niemöller, the founder of the Pastor's Emergency League, was arrested in July and remained in detention for eight years.[22]

---

[22] Ibid., 579.

After the closing of the Confessing seminaries, the work of training ordinands continued under the name of the collective pastorates. This was a system in which young men were appointed as apprentices to the ministry under the supervision of already established ministers in the Confessing Church. Dietrich would share time between his two groups of young men now in the towns of Köslin and Schlawe. The latter group eventually moved to Gross-Schlönwitz, and then to an empty farmhouse in Sigurdshof. During those days, Bonhoeffer travelled much between groups of students and also to Berlin on various matters connected with the Confessing Church. His life was characterized by an unsettled existence.[23]

In the growing euphoria for the Führer after the Austrian *Anschluss* [annexation] Dr. Friedrich Werner, president of the Evangelical High Church Council, prepared a special birthday present for Hitler on April 20, 1938. All pastors in the Evangelical Church were to swear a loyalty oath to Hitler : "I swear that I will be loyal and obedient to Adolf Hitler, the Leader of the German Reich and people...."[24] The taking of this oath was, of course, on pain of employment as a pastor. Dietrich was exempt since he was not officially classified as a pastor. However, great debate and anguish of soul followed in the confessing Church. Great majorities in the various church districts voted in favor of taking the oath. Karl Barth reproved the church from Basel, Switzerland, and asked why they were gambling the future credibility of the Confessing Church. When this

[23] Ibid., 594.
[24] Wind, 129.

shameful episode ended, Nazi leader Martin Bormann communicated to church leaders that the oath was purely voluntary on the part of the pastors and not required by the state. One can imagine the soul-sickness that many felt upon experiencing this cynical and masterful manipulation by the Nazis. This event together with the Church's silence after the November 9, 1938 *Kristallnacht* (or the night of broken glass, which started the pogrom against the Jews) began to isolate Dietrich from what was left of the Confessing Church.

In the margin of his Bible, Dietrich wrote 9/11/38 beside Psalm 74:8-9, which he underlined: "they burned all the meeting places of God in the land. We do not see our signs; there is no longer any prophet and there is none among us who knows how long."

Because of the immediate threat of war and Bonhoeffer's conscientious objection, he sought and received an invitation to lecture at Union Theological Seminary, where he had done his post-doctoral work. He departed on June 2, 1939. On board the ship Bremen, he wrote; "We ought to be found only where He is. We can no longer, in fact, be anywhere else than where He is. Whether it is you working over there or I working in America, we are all only where He is. He takes us with him. Or have I, after all, avoided the place where He is? The place where He is for me?" Dietrich was not attempting to formulate a law as to what Christians may or may not do under persecution. He did not think it un-Christian to try and avoid persecution [the Church Fathers would agree]. He came to realize that he could not do so and that his decision to come to the U.S. had been a mistake.[25] In a letter to Reinhold Niebuhr he stated that; "the Christians of Germany would have to make a decision between wanting the victory of their nation, and the death of a Christian civilization, or the defeat of their nation and the survival of a Christian civilization. You cannot... remain out of a country when your fellow Christians face such a momentous issue."[26] His decision was made to return to Germany, and he arrived in Berlin on July 27.

After the invasion of Poland the German armies went from success to success. The British and French declared war on September 3, 1939. World War II had begun. This raised a question as to what the church should do to resist an outwardly successful regime in which political murder and concentration camps were the norm. This time frame provides the context for a section in his later book, *Ethics*, called The Idolization of Success in which success becomes self-justifying and morally right by definition. The Hitler regime shows us how deceived we can be at that point.

As the grip of the state became stronger, many citizens found it safer not to know many things that were going on in the Third Reich. Bonhoeffer desired to be politically informed. He felt it was part of his responsibility for the future of the Church and Germany. He began a friendship with Hans von Dohnanyi, who frequented the Bonhoeffer's house in Berlin. Von Dohnanyi was a brilliant jurist, never part of any National Socialist organizations, and eventual private secretary to Admiral Wilhelm Canaris, who was head

---

[25] Ibid., 137.

[26] Reinhold Niebuhr, "To America and Back," *I Knew Dietrich Bonhoeffer*, ed. Wolf-Dieter Zimmermann (New York: Harper & Row, 1966), 165.

of Germany's counter-intelligence service, the *Abwehr*. It was as a member of this group that von Dohnanyi became an integral part of conspiracy plots to overthrow Hitler.

Bonhoeffer was privy to their discussions. One evening von Dohnanyi asked him to comment on Matthew 26:52 "all who take the sword will perish by the sword." Dietrich replied that this was true for the circle of conspirators as well, but that the times called for men to take up that responsibility.[27] Bonhoeffer's actions during the war may seem contradictory to his earlier teaching and stance against the regime, but they were not. For instance, he concurred with the advice given to Martin Niemöller that he should volunteer for the navy. This would appear to support the Hitler regime, but the reasoning was that Niemöller would get out of prison and be in a position of responsibility and authority in the event of a coup d'etat.

The announcement that France had capitulated came while Dietrich was in a café with Eberhard Bethge. The patrons went wild with joy, and Dietrich gave the straight-arm Hitler salute to which Bethge asked, "Are you crazy?" "We shall have to run risks for very different things now, but not for that salute!" replied Dietrich.[28]

Bonhoeffer's move from pacifism to conspirator was not as puzzling as it seems at first glance. He was zealous for the truth of the gospel and the freedom to preach the gospel. In light of those overarching goals, Bonhoeffer's actions were responses to the situation at hand and a response to the will of God. In a more basic way the question is "What does it

---

[27] Bethge, 625.
[28] Ibid., 681.

mean to be a disciple of Christ?" To this question, Bonhoeffer's life gives us an unusual picture. Certainly the unique people that he knew gave him entrance into the conspiracy against Hitler. Most Christians in Germany were not in that position.

Emmi Bonhoeffer (the wife of Klaus, Dietrich's brother) related her question to Dietrich and his response, "How is that with you Christians? You will not kill, but that another one does it; you agree, and you are glad about it—how is that?" Dietrich replied, "One shouldn't be glad about it, but I understand what you mean. It is out of the question for a Christian to ask someone else to do the dirty work so that he can keep his own hands clean. If one sees that something needs to be done, then one must be prepared to do it whether one is a Christian or not. If one sees the task as necessary according to one's own conscience."

"If I see that a madman is driving a car into a group of innocent bystanders, then I can't as a Christian simply wait for the catastrophe and comfort the wounded and bury the dead. I must try to wrest the steering wheel out of the hands of the madman."

Emmi Bonhoeffer analyzed this moment: "That's the way he came into the conspiracy. It's not a break in his life that he was first a pacifist and first a pious child, and then a helpful young man and later on suddenly he became a politician. It's a quite clear line, going through; but the situations changed and the tasks changed."[29]

After he became involved in the resistance as a courier for the Abwehr, Dietrich could no longer involve his brethren

---

[29] *Dietrich Bonhoeffer: Memories and Perspectives*, Trinity Films, 1983.

from the Confessing Movement. This was a path he had to tread alone. The ethical question for him became the toleration of the Hitler government, which meant to tacitly participate in mass murder, or to be willing to acquiesce in the assassination of Hitler himself. This is certainly not a pleasant situation for anyone. From here there is no escape into a region of ideas or of theology for theology's sake, but the theology of the deed becomes the compelling motivation. There is also no escape into an ethically neutral zone or into a zone in which no sin is involved. "The new turning point demanded an entirely different sacrifice: the sacrifice of his Christian reputation."[30]

On September 4, 1940, Bonoeffer was forbidden to speak publicly anywhere in the Reich, and was ordered to report his movements to the police. His work in military intelligence for the *Abwehr*, however, provided him with acceptable cover for his continued travels throughout Germany and abroad. He met with several of his old contacts in the ecumenical movement with the purpose of getting a message to higher circles of the Allies that a true resistance existed in Germany. Bonhoeffer spent four weeks at this time beginning his work, *Ethics*. General Hans Oster and Dohnanyi decided that an official residence address for Dietrich in Munich would be advantageous. His relative, Countess Kalckreuth, who lived in Munich allowed Dietrich to establish nominal residence there. The Military Intelligence Office in the meantime found residence for Bonhoeffer in the Franciscan monastery in Ettal, where he

---

[30] Bethge, 678.

found a few uninterrupted months to continue the work on *Ethics*.

In the deteriorating political situation in Germany, Jews were gathered on October 16, 1941, at the Levetzowstrasse synagogue for deportation. Prior to this time Hans von Dohnanyi and the other members of the *Abwehr* circle had begun a plan known as Operation Seven. It was a plan to use seven Jews as phony agents of the *Abwehr* in order to get them into Switzerland. This plan, in which Dietrich was involved, required much intrigue and subterfuge, but it was eventually successful in getting fourteen Jews into Switzerland in the Fall of 1942. In prison later, Bonhoeffer would be interrogated about this affair.[31]

Dietrich was able to meet with the Bishop of Chichester, George Bell, in Sigtuna, Sweden in May, 1942. Bonhoeffer again discussed the resistance and had a list of names of people who would probably be involved in forming a new government when the expected coup took place. Bell continued to make the case to the Allied authorities that there was a difference between Hitler and the German people, but the Allies were silent on this subject. Dietrich took his leave of the Bishop of Chichester: "This spirit of fellowship and of Christian brotherliness will carry me through the darkest hours, and even if things go worse than we hope and expect, the light of these few days will never extinguish in my heart....I shall think of you on Wednesday. Please pray for us."[32] George Bell continued to expend himself on behalf of the conspirators. He tried to bring their

[31] Ibid., 749.
[32] Ibid., 762-763.

case before the British and Allied authorities, but met with limited success.

In a letter to Eberhard Bethge, Bonhoeffer wrote of the change of perspective he was experiencing, and the toll the conspiracy was taking upon him. "My activities, which have lately been very much in the worldly sector, give me plenty to think about. I am surprised that I live, and can go on living, for days without the Bible....When I open the Bible again, it is ever so new and cheering....I know that I only need to open my own books to hear what there is to be said against all this....But I feel how my resistance to everything 'religious' is growing....I am not religious by nature. But I always have to be thinking of God and of Christ, and I set great store by genuineness, life, freedom and compassion. Only I find the religious trappings so uncomfortable. Do you understand?"[33] Bonhoeffer was beginning to live the religionless Christianity that he speculated upon in his *Letters and Papers from Prison.*

The conspiracy centering around General Beck, Admiral Canaris, Hans Oster, Dohnanyi and Bonhoeffer continued. On March 12, 1943, Hans von Dohnanyi delivered some explosives in a briefcase to one of the officers in the conspiracy, Henning von Tresckow (the other officer involved in this plot was Fabian von Schlabrendorff). They were to be used to take down an airplane with Hitler aboard. The explosives didn't fire. In another attempt very shortly afterward, Major von Gersdorff was to accompany Hitler in an automobile carrying two bombs in his briefcase for use at a military celebration. Hitler left the celebration after ten

---

[33] Wind, 153.

minutes before any attempt was made.[34] These were two of the many attempts made on Hitler's life.

On January 17, 1943, Dietrich became engaged to the lovely Maria von Wedemeyer, granddaughter of his great friend, Ruth von Kleist-Retzow. The public announcement of their engagement was to be delayed for a time, but the announcement was made public shortly thereafter upon Dietrich's arrest. On April 5, 1943, both von Dohnanyi and Bonhoeffer were arrested by Judge Advocate Manfred Roeder and Gestapo Comissioner Sonderegger. They were taken to Tegel prison in the northwestern area of Berlin. Dr. Roeder was notorious for his investigations. He had broken up one resistance group in 1943, and as a result seventy-five death sentences were handed out, including one to Arvid Harnack, the nephew of Bonhoeffer's old theology professor Adolf von Harnack.[35]

The Gestapo suspected the activities of Admiral Canaris' office and hoped to find out more through Dohnanyi and Bonhoeffer. However, no further information was obtained from them. There was not enough evidence to charge them with treason or to use torture, and plausible explanations for their actions were always produced by the two friends. They were able to communicate secretly during those days.

The interrogation of Bonhoeffer followed four themes. These were the same topics under which von Dohnanyi was interrogated. The first was Bonhoeffer's military exemption as being necessary for the war effort. The second was his work in Operation Seven used for the movement of fourteen

---

[34] Bethge, 148.
[35] Ibid., 157.

Jews to Switzerland including a good friend and member of the Confessing Church, Charlotte Friedenthal. The third heading was Dietrich's foreign journeys, which were expected to be unrelated to any meaningful military intelligence. The fourth theme was a discussion of military exemptions for officials in the Confessing Church. Both von Dohnanyi and Bonhoeffer satisfied their interrogators on these points.[36]

In June, 1943, Dietrich and Maria were able to meet again in person under the surveillance of Dr. Roeder. Writing privileges were extended, and Dietrich's emotional life was helped greatly by this interaction with his fiancée. Poetry followed with expressions of love, grief, torment, and faith. Some poems were written to Maria. Some were sent to Eberhard Bethge. While imprisoned in Tegel, Dietrich was able to establish relationships with other prisoners who were waiting interrogation. Bethge reports that "He tried to do something for them or to bring some pleasure into their lives."[37]

Count Klaus von Stauffenberg continued the conspiracy against Hitler after the breakup of the Canaris, Oster, von Dohnanyi group. On July 20, 1944, he was able to get a briefcase with explosives placed fairly close to Hitler at a meeting with the generals in East Prussia. Von Stauffenberg had been able to arm only half of the explosives. The bomb went off, destroying the bunker, and several generals were killed while Hitler was only wounded. He vowed to kill all the members of the conspiracy. In October, 1944, the

---

[36] Ibid., 814.
[37] Ibid., 849.

Gestapo found Dohnanyi's documents and dossier on the activities of the Third Reich at Zossen. These Zossen papers also reported the conspiratorial activities of the Abwehr. Thus, the fate of von Dohnanyi and Bonhoeffer was effectively sealed.

In his last days, Dietrich was transferred to the Reich Security Prison in Berlin on Prinz Albrecht Strasse, where further interrogation by the Gestapo took place. The discovery of the Zossen papers gave him a reprieve for a few months as Reich Security became interested in continuing questioning concerning the circles of the conspirators. On February 7, 1945, Dietrich was taken to the concentration camp at Buchenwald, where he met British Captain Payne Best, who gives a good report of his last days, describing him as all humility and sweetness. "He always seemed to diffuse an atmosphere of happiness, of joy in every smallest event in life, and a deep gratitude for the mere fact that he was alive....He was one of the very few men I have ever met to whom his God was real and ever close to him."[38]

The van, in which Bonhoeffer and other "special" prisoners were transported to the extermination camp at Flossenbürg, broke down outside of the town of Regensburg. The prisoners were then taken to the village of Schönberg and kept locked in a school building there. It was in Schönberg that Dietrich held his final worship service with his fellow prisoners. His texts were from Isaiah 53; "By His stripes we are healed," and 1 Peter; "Blessed be the God and Father of our Lord Jesus Christ. By God's great mercy we have been born anew to a living hope through the

---

[38] Bethge, 920.

resurrection of Jesus Christ from the dead." In this dark situation Bonhoeffer was able to reach the hearts of all the men by finding just the right words and the right thoughts.

The next day Dietrich Bonhoeffer was hanged for high treason at the Flossenbürg concentration camp, Monday, April 9, 1945. His last recorded words were "This is the end, for me the beginning of life. I believe in universal Christian brotherhood which rises above national interests and I believe that our victory is certain." He requested that Captain Best convey those words to George Bell, the Bishop of Chichester.[39]

---

[39] Ibid., 927.

CHAPTER 2

ETHICS

AS A PROFESSOR of business ethics at a small Christian liberal arts school, I have wondered many times if there is anything different in my presentation of business ethics from a presentation given by an atheist or a person from any other belief system. Obviously, there are many people who act with a high degree of integrity in business situations who do not practice the Christian faith. There are keen ethicists who can dissect the many ramifications of an ethical situation. The whole concept, therefore, of business ethics from a Christian standpoint becomes problematical. This approach to business ethics is a specific instance of the general problem of Christian ethics which Dietrich Bonhoeffer treats in his book, *Ethics.*

Ethics was written in moments of quiet meditation at the Franciscan monastery of Ettal in Bavaria. Ettal is located just over the hill and around a curve in the road from Oberammergau the site of the famous passion play. The time of retreat and lying low was worked out on Dietrich's behalf by his superiors in the *Abwehr*. It was also written in moments of hurry during his travels, and it was written in prison. It is really a long series of meditations rather than a carefully finished product. It is a fragment. However, this fragment along with *Letters and Papers from Prison*, which is a collection of letters, is largely responsible for his growing reputation.

In *Ethics*, Bonhoeffer provides us with a new perspective. He makes us think. He brings something unique to the discussion of ethics as a Christian. In the darkening situation in Germany that Bonhoeffer faced after his return from America in 1939 he said, "To want to be only a Christian, a timeless disciple—that now became a costly privilege. To become engaged for his times, where he stood, was far more open to misinterpretation, less glorious, more confined. Yet this alone was what it now meant to be a Christian."[1] Bonhoeffer was writing and living *Ethics* simultaneously in a crucible of violence, intrigue, cynicism, deceit, and horror. In *Ethics*, Bonhoeffer leaves us the writings of one who was trying to live as a true disciple of Christ in the Third Reich. I will attempt to apply his *Ethics,* and his other works as well, to an examination of some themes from business ethics. This may provide a different way of thinking about this vast and important topic.

In *Ethics*, Bonhoeffer begins before the Fall with man's uninterrupted relationship with God. In that situation man knew only good. No confusion or hesitancy of decision-

---

[1] Eberhard Bethge, *Dietrich Bonhoeffer: A Biography*, (Minneapolis, MN: Fortress Press, 2000), 678.

making was present. Sin then enters the world, and our knowledge of good and evil begins. Therefore, "...Christian ethics discerns a falling away from the origin."[2] Ethics is an attempt to think through our new relationship with God and with other human beings after the Fall. It is not a prideful study, but one undertaken with humility given our experiential knowledge of evil and the struggle we encounter in "doing justice, loving mercy, and walking humbly with God." Humility is the order of the day since even the voice of our conscience is problematic. Before the Fall there was no conscience. Conscience came into existence with the Fall and is therefore part of the Fall. Conscience deals with the permitted and the forbidden. It does not embrace the whole of life like the Word or the Commandment of God, and it is concerned basically with man's relation with himself—to his better self. Although conscience can provide an important warning about various actions, we need to be careful. When conscience pretends to be the voice of God, it may, in fact, be the voice of the devil.[3]

Fundamental Problem of Business Ethics

THERE SEEMS to be in the presentation of university business ethics the interminable discussion of cases and the correct ethical resolution of these cases. This is standard

---

[2] Dietrich Bonhoeffer, *Ethics* (New York: Touchstone, 1995), 21.
[3] Dietrich Bonhoeffer, *London, 1933-1935*, DBWE Vol. 13 (Minneapolis: Fortress Press, 2007), 315.

pedagogy. It is probably beneficial to the students to read some cases that have subtle ethical decision-making involved or blatant wrongs which were unopposed by the whole organization. The cases of blatant wrong raise questions of will and courage, as in, "Why didn't someone do the right thing?" Courage, from the derivation of its name, has something to do with the heart. If students' hearts are strengthened for doing good, casework can be appropriately applauded. The standard of good in many of these cases is evident. There is usually no big mystery as to the right course of action.

The ethical imperative here is straightforward. One should do good and avoid evil. Who could object? Perhaps more subtly, we might say, one should be good by doing good. In other words, the results of these discussions are that one should be good and do good. However, here Bonhoeffer states that we are back in the old self-centered ethic.

> If the ethical problem presents itself essentially in the form of enquiries about one's own being good and doing good, this means that it has already been decided that it is the self and the world which are the ultimate reality. The aim of all ethical reflection is, then, that I myself shall be good and that the world shall become good through my action. But the problem of ethics at once assumes a new aspect if it becomes apparent that these realities, myself and the world, themselves lie imbedded in a quite different ultimate reality, namely, the reality of God, the Creator, Reconciler and Redeemer. What is of ultimate importance is now no longer that I should become good, or that the condition of the world would be made better by my action, but that the reality of God should show itself everywhere to be the ultimate reality. Where there is faith in God as the ultimate

reality, all concern with ethics will have as its starting-point that God shows Himself to be good, even if this involves the risk that I myself and the world are not good but thoroughly bad.[4]

Business ethics in dealing with commercial activity in all its forms admits that we have fallen away from our original relationship with God and that we are in an intense relationship with the world, i.e. the fallen world. Therefore, any attempt to impose millennium-like notions upon the world of business must be rejected at the outset. At the Fanø ecumenical conference in Denmark in 1934, Bonhoeffer made clear his view that the whole political-economic nexus would never bring world peace. Does peace come about, "...Through a system of political treaties? Through the investment of international capital in different countries? Through the big banks, through money? Or through universal peaceful rearmament in order to guarantee peace? Through none of these, for the single reason that in all of them peace is confused with safety.... peace must be dared. It is the great venture."[5]

The world of business is apart from God in the sense that we are apart from God since the Fall. It is from this sober assessment of humankind's condition that the discussion of ethics proceeds. "Man's life is now disunion with God, with men, with things, and with himself." [6] A burgeoning economy does not indicate peace with God, unity with other men, nor internal or external peace. These topics have been

[4] Bonhoeffer, *London*, 186-187.
[5] Bonhoeffer, *London*, 308-309.
[6] Bonhoeffer, *Ethics*, 24.

broached many years ago by the exemplar in economic studies, Adam Smith. Through publication of his famous book *The Wealth of Nations* in 1776, the contribution of free markets to the welfare of mankind has become more commonly understood.

Adam Smith
& Modern Economic Thought

THERE IS NOTHING unique to the Christian faith or discipleship in Adam Smith's shrewd comment on wise behavior given our human condition; "It is not from the benevolence of the butcher, the brewer, or the baker, that we expect our dinner, but from their regard to their own interest. We address ourselves, not to their humanity but to their self-love, and never talk to them of our own necessities but of their advantages."[7] This common-sense observation of economic interest in ourselves and others provides a generalization of human behavior through which economics and the business school explains, makes predictions, and otherwise does its work.

From Smith, also, the business school has received the doctrine of the Invisible Hand. This doctrine states that through the extension of liberty, individuals will pursue their self-interest in terms of business endeavors, vocations,

---

[7] Adam Smith, *An Inquiry into the Nature and Causes of the Wealth of Nations*, Vol. I (Chicago: The University of Chicago Press, 1976), 18

etc., and that this pursuit will produce a greater social good than any other organization of production.

Smith is making a practical and pragmatic point concerning wise government policy with respect to fostering abundant production. Adam Smith was a moral philosopher and economist, not a theologian. It is true, however, that the term "Invisible Hand," sounds like the doctrine of providence in which God is working things out for our good and His glory. The idea of markets spontaneously producing order or social good is tied to the idea of providence.[8] This presents us with one of the puzzles of business ethics. How can selfish living produce personal good or societal good? I think two answers can be provided. The first is that our work life and consumption has a large, loving component. This is not very often emphasized given the self-interest assumption of economics, but economist-historian, Deirdre McCloskey makes the following comment:

> ...the economy cannot actually get along without a good deal of love. Over half of consumer purchases at point of sale, for example, are on behalf of children and husbands and mothers and friends. Love runs consumption. Feminist economists have been noting for some time that without such love, and therefore without such altruistic purchases, the human race would promptly die out. A theory based on selfishness alone therefore cannot work scientifically.[9]

---

[8] José Lopez and José Santos, "Smithian Perspective on the Markets of Beliefs," *Journal of Markets and Morality* 11 (1) Spring, 2008 64.

[9] Deirdre N. McCloskey, *The Bourgeois Virtues*, (Chicago: University of Chicago Press, 2006), 56-57.

The self-interest assumption has been overworked and pushed to some kind of extreme. The second answer concerns the providence of God. God is ruler over the fallen world. The world is given to us for our benefit, for our enjoyment, as well as the venue for our discipleship. Why wouldn't God's providence work through markets to produce some good for the participants, the non-participants, believers and unbelievers alike? God's providence could produce some good through planned or controlled markets also. God's providence is operable in our world. Markets are clearly part of the world as we know it, and Christ has stated that His followers are "in the world, but not of it." We are situated within work and within markets, apparently with Christ's approbation.

Regardless of the theological framework in Smith, the policy implication is clear. Allow the individual entrepreneur to evaluate his business in terms of pricing, investment in capital equipment, expansion, etc. No government bureau can do as effective a job in this as the individual businessperson. "[The businessperson]...by directing that industry in such a manner as its produce may be of the greatest value, he intends only his own gain, and he is in this, as in many other cases, led by an invisible hand to promote an end which was no part of his intention." [10]

Francis Hutcheson, Adam Smith's professor at Glasgow, took a benign or providential view of God's action through the economy by saying: "Such is the goodness of God to us, that the most useful and necessary things are generally very

---

[10] Smith, 477.

plentiful and easily acquired" [11] Both of these men, Hutcheson and Smith occupied the chair of moral philosophy at the University of Glasgow. In the course of their lectures they discussed the economic activity that is proper to human beings as part of their study of moral philosophy. Business and economic studies began through a discussion of the moral and ethical dimension of human life.

Our Present Condition

THE CARICATURE of economic man, a person who pursues maximum profits or wages or money returns in every situation, pushes ethical considerations into the background in modern economics studies. Efficient and increasing production seems to be the primary focus. However, physical provision, no matter how great, does not necessarily bring friendship with other people nor union with God. We live in a fallen world from which we do not withdraw. Its fallenness is not only accepted as a given, but is demonstrated to us over and over again through our own unkindness, petty actions, cutting words, and gossip. Our actions are reciprocated by others so that life in the workplace can become a battle.

We accept the guilt of the world as our guilt since we are also involved in wrong action in the workplace. Through

---

[11] Francis Hutcheson, *A Short Introduction to Moral Philosophy* (Hildesheim: George Oms Verlagsbuchhandlung, 1971), 28.

this acknowledgement and acceptance of guilt we are able to live authentic lives rather than inauthentic ones.[12] How is the world's guilt my guilt? Bonhoeffer explained this in one of his London sermons preached immediately after the Röhm putsch of July 1, 1934, in which possibly more than 200 people were murdered by the Nazis. This event was a triumph of intrigue and murder by Hitler in his pursuit of absolute power in Germany. Ernst Röhm was the leader of Hitler's SA troops (storm troopers), a street-brawling paramilitary group. They were used mainly to intimidate Communist groups in Germany, but their usefulness to Hitler came to an end when the German military and industrial leaders began to complain about them. Hitler met with President Paul von Hindenberg, now in failing health, and Defense Minister Blomberg and was stiffly informed that the SA problem must be solved or the president would simply declare martial law and let the German Army run the country, effectively ending the Nazi regime. In order to stay in President Hindenberg's good graces, Hitler had the elite SS troops execute many of the SA troops' top leaders in the so-called "night of the long knives." Hitler's long-time friend, Röhm, was also murdered.

Shortly following this event, Bonhoeffer preached to his London congregation on the murder of some Galileans by Pilate. It seems that these Galileans had been killed in the domain of the Temple itself for being, perhaps, some kind of rabble-rousers. Jesus asked them, "Do you think that these Galileans were worse sinners than all other Galilieans,

---

[12] Dietrich Bonhoeffer, *Act and Being*, DBWE Vol. 2 (Minneapolis: Fortress Press, 1996), 70.

because they suffered in this way? No, I tell you; but unless you repent, you will all likewise perish."[13] In the sermon, Dietrich related a story from the life of Gandhi to illustrate the acceptance of guilt which leads to repentance. It seems that while Gandhi was directing a school, a shocking injustice was done among the students. Rather than reproving any student, Gandhi saw this as a call for repentance on his part. He went into a period of fasting and self-denial. He saw in his students' guilt his own guilt and his lack of love. Faith, hope and love could be found only through repentance.[14]

Surely there will be further revelations of wrongdoing in business at both the individual and corporate levels. Who is guilty? Perhaps we need to think more soberly. It is not the earning of a living by bosses and employees that brings businesses down, but in many cases, greed. In fact, greed and corruption can bring governments down. The collapse of credit markets in the fall of 2008 is a good example of egregious behavior on several fronts.

For years US administrations have pressured banks to make home loans to people with obviously weak credit. Many of the banks and financial institutions cooperated. Cheap credit led to a housing bubble with rapidly rising home prices which provided an environment where real estate speculators (and otherwise normal homeowners) could make some easy money. The bubble eventually burst with at least a five trillion dollar loss in housing values. This fiasco

13 Luke 13:2-3.
14 Bonhoeffer, *London*, 370.

resulted in a world-wide credit crisis and recession. Greed for votes and greed for money caused this disaster.

Another interesting result of the 2008 financial crisis was the revealing of "normative" Wall Street corporate compensation policies. Top executives from Wall Street's principal performers were seen to receive year-end compensation packages ranging from $25-48 million and many of these executives walked out of the financial crisis with golden parachutes (severance packages) worth up to $25 million. Greed at the top reflects and produces greed at the bottom.

Contrary to Michael Douglas' famous speech in the movie *Wall Street*, greed is not good. Greed is sin. "Thou shalt not covet." Greed is different than depending on God for our daily bread through work, and greed dwells in the heart. This is clear speech from God. Perhaps it is not the captains of industry who need to be converted but us. In following this line of thought Bonhoeffer further illustrates this point in discussion with several of his friends. These colleagues had made various proposals concerning the need to visit Hitler and discuss various theological issues with him leading to a resolution of the church struggle. Dietrich responded in a letter to his friend Erwin Sutz. "The Oxford Movement was naïve enough to try to convert Hitler—a laughable failure to understand what is really happening—it is we who ought to be converted, not Hitler...." [15] Bonhoeffer continues in the same July sermon:

---

[15] Bethge, 358.

Jesus too raises the question of guilt. But he answers it differently. It is not Pilate or the Galileans who are meant here, but we, we ourselves. In the face of terrible human catastrophes, Christians are not to assume the arrogant, know-all attitude of looking on and judging, but rather are to recognize: this is the fruit of what I and my brothers have sown—and these people here, these Galileans and Pilate, are my brothers, my brothers in sin, in hate and evil and lovelessness, my brothers in guilt. Whatever happens to them is meant for me too; they are only showing my God's finger pointed in anger, pointed at me as well. So let us repent and realize our guilt and not judge.[16]

The Four Mandates

BUSINESS ETHICS once again focuses our thinking on a part of the original source of our disciplines, namely, the Chair of Moral Philosophy. Business ethics is *par excellence* a discussion of life in this world. Bonhoeffer's emphasis on the "this-worldliness" of Christianity should fit in well with our journey through this most worldly of endeavors—business. "One must live through the tension between being a Christian and being in the world if one is to avoid the mere spouting of empty religious phrases."[17]

The Fall brings us back to a view of the disunion that exists between human beings in all our social relationships. There is a certain lack of love in our actions, or might we say an excess of self-love? Self-love is love, but it is love gone

---

[16] Ibid., 369.
[17] Georg Huntemann, *Dietrich Bonhoeffer: An Evangelical Reassessment* (Grand Rapids, MI: Baker Books, 1993), 73.

wrong. It is love that has fallen away from the origin, which is, the perfect love of God. Perhaps the enlightened self-interest assumption of economics models is not enlightened enough. "It is self-satisfied...a love that is really hatred of God and my brother and sister, because they could only disturb me within the tight little circle I have drawn around myself. It has all the same power, the same passion, the same exclusiveness of real love—here or there. What is totally different is its goal—myself, rather than God and my neighbor."[18]

However, the very structure of life gives us tasks to perform which are other-oriented. These tasks move us along in our knowledge of God. Bonhoeffer presents these tasks to us under four headings. They are labor, marriage, government and church. These four things are mandates from God to us. These mandates follow from the creation accounts, the Book of Ecclesiastes and New Testament teaching. In the early chapters of Genesis we are given the joy of manhood and womanhood by direct creation. As such, it is man and woman in the one-flesh relationship that bear the image of God. Marriage is thus established. Next comes the command to dress and keep the garden, and the joy of work is established. The authority of God is implicit also as governor and ruler over humankind. The mandate of church more clearly derives from New Testament teaching, but can also be derived from worship accounts in the Book of Genesis.

The book of Ecclesiastes with its theme of vanity also gives us a theme of human joy. There is joy to be

---

[18] Bonhoeffer, *London*, 382.

experienced in this vain world. Some of the benefits proper to human life are discussed by Bonhoeffer in "The Right to Bodily Life."[19] In this life and the next, man exists and will exist in a body. This is Christian teaching. The body then has its own inherent dignity, right to be preserved, and joy. Life in the body is a means to an end and an end in itself. There are certain joys that are naturally appropriate to the body, and God has placed His stamp of approval upon them. By way of analogy, the joys of bodily life are a reminder of the joys of heavenly life. The wise man in Ecclesiastes mentions the joy of good food and good drink, the joy of married life, and the joy of good work. These things come to men and women from the hand of God. Bonhoeffer discusses these mandates as tracks that God has given every person on which to run. We can engage in these activities with a good conscience and a good will because God has given these things to us.

These four mandates, including the mandate of church, bring concreteness to theological discussion. They are given not to cause men and women to live divided lives, but participation in all these areas lead to wholeness. "It was precisely concreteness that Bonhoeffer endeavored to realize. That is why he always saw the writing of a work on ethics as his main task in life. He wanted to articulate the concrete significance of Christian faith for living the Christian life in his day."[20] The four tracks are interrelated. They are not meant to divide us up, but to contribute to the development of a whole person. We shall look briefly at the mandates of

---

[19] Bonhoeffer, *Ethics*, 154-157.
[20] Huntemann, 65.

government, marriage and labor. The mandate of the church shall be treated at length in the following chapter.

Government

GOVERNMENT IS NOT [or should not be] a creative institution but a preserving institution. Government protects the other spheres of life; namely marriage, labor and church. Government has an interest in marriage and is the guarantor of it. Any society has an interest in the health, well-being, and education of its children. One of the purposes here being precisely to care for and educate the next generation. Government itself does not produce value. Labor and the business enterprise do produce value. "The governing authority must never itself try to become the subject, the driving force, in this domain of labour; for this would be to imperil gravely both the divine mandate of labour and its own divine mandate." [21] Government does not become the driving force behind labor and business, but it supports them by exercising its coercive power to enforce contracts and provide a legal framework in which the creative process may flourish.

The formation and institution of government was considered by the ancients to arise from the nature of man, from natural law. The state or *polis* was the highest expression of the culture of a people or a nation. All values

---

[21]Bonhoeffer, *Ethics*, 207.

had meaning in reference to the *polis*. Thus, Socrates died willingly rather than be separated from the *polis* through an arranged escape from detention. Bonhoeffer argues that the state as a cultural expression of the will of the people made its way into German thinking and theology by way of the philosophy of Hegel, perhaps Germany's most well known Idealist philosopher, who begins his system with humans living in an immediate and simple relation to nature. Hegel was primarily concerned with the synthesizing of the individual with overarching wholes such as the universal will. Thus in relation to politics, the individual is subsumed by the whole, that is, the state which is "the highest expression of objective Spirit" or truth.[22] From this view of the state it is easy to see in Hegel's writings that the State plays a divine role in history, although he did not deny historical failures.

Therefore, with the multiplication and satisfaction of human desires, a whole complex of economic and political relationships arises. The state, then, with its highest expression through the legislature, is like a community, and government becomes the initiator of culture and economy. The problem here is that human community operates through love and largely through voluntarism. Unlike community, government must exercise force and coercion to maintain order. When this occurs it becomes evident that government is using these tools to preserve culture and community, not to form culture and community. Bonhoeffer states concerning government, "Whenever the

---

[22] Frederick J. Coppleston, *A History of Philosophy: Volume VII: Modern Philosophy* (New York: Image Books, 1994), 212.

state becomes the executor of all the vital and cultural activities of man, it forfeits its own proper dignity, its specific authority as government."[23]

Government, however, is instituted by God. It was made necessary by the Fall. Even before the Fall, Adam had a law, but there was no need for coercive power because of his total obedience. Sin also brought with it the need for the coercive power of government. Like the other mandates, government does not lose its divine ordinance or dignity because of a failure of policy or an ethical failure of one of its officials. Therefore, government retains its mandate apart from the character of the persons who are governing. The idea of a Christian state is not necessary. Government officials are God's ministers (Romans 13:1) whether they are Christians or not.

The goal of government, as with the other mandates, is to serve Jesus Christ. Government is not necessarily Christian, but it does not exclude Christ. It fulfills its task by taking seriously the contents of the last five of the Ten Commandments, namely, "Do not kill", "Do not commit adultery", Do not steal", "Do not bear false witness", "Do not covet". Government knows these commandments primarily from the preaching of the church. Even in countries without a vigorous Christian presence, these prohibitions are known from nature and experience. Here, Bonhoeffer allows the possibility of natural law informing human beings outside of the revelation of Christ. However,

---

[23] Bonhoeffer, *Ethics*, 329.

he argues that natural law has its foundation in Jesus Christ.[24]

In discussions of government, the question is raised as to when it is appropriate to disobey. Bonhoeffer also deals with this question. In almost all cases, obedience is required. There may be cases in which the citizen is doubtful as to his obedience, but civil disobedience requires a clear denying by government of its divine commission. What might be an example of this? In a prescient passage as to his own involvement in the conspiracy to overthrow Hitler, Bonhoeffer states, "...if government violates or exceeds its commission at any point, for example by making itself master over the belief of the congregation, then at this point, indeed, obedience is to be refused, for conscience' sake, for the Lord's sake."[25]

The Third Reich's interference in the doctrinal integrity of the church compelled Dietrich to become involved in the long, convoluted church struggle (*Kirchenkampf*). Later, he became involved in the conspiracy itself. However, at the same time, he paid taxes, obeyed orders of the police and other laws of the state. In other words, the government hadn't been completely demonized. The complete demonization of government occurs only at the time of the end with government embodying Antichrist. Then, there is a separation between the congregation and a government which has renounced its divine commission. "The mission of government consists in serving the dominion of Christ on

[24] Bonhoeffer, *Ethics*, 336.
[25] Bonhoeffer, *Ethics*, 338.

earth by the exercise of the worldly power of the sword and of justice."[26]

Marriage and Labor as Divine Institutions

MARRIAGE IS GIVEN to us from the beginning. Man and woman hold this mandate of marriage from God regardless of the historical development of marriage or the various cultural forms which it might take. The great blessing of bringing forth new life is bestowed upon husband and wife. The parents act as deputies for the child, educating him and training him. The parents represent God to the child. This is their concrete task given to them by God.

Marriage also represents the great mystery of the relationship between Christ and the Church as the Apostle Paul teaches. The goal of marriage is not only procreation of new lives for the service of Jesus Christ, but the glorification of God directly through the mystery of the interaction of husband and wife in imitation of Christ and His Church. The bodily joy of sexual union is in view here also, which in an analogous way points to the joy within the Trinity.

In saying that marriage is a mandate given by God to all people, Bonhoeffer is obviously aware of the vocation of singleness (He was single). Even as single people, we are related to other people through the family. There are a lot of personal relationships that simply come with the territory as a result of marriage. He is simply saying that marriage is

---

[26] Bonhoeffer, *Ethics*, 335.

given to us by God; it has a purpose and a goal (the glorification of Christ); and that all people are related to it and affected by it in some way.

"The divine character of labour cannot be ascribed to its general usefulness or its intrinsic values, but only to its origin, its continuance and its goal in Jesus Christ... labour....for the fulfillment of the divine task and purpose is divine."[27] So what is the divine task and purpose for which we are working in the business world? The instruction to dress and keep the garden is given to Adam in Chapter 2 of Genesis, so that work itself is not a punishment for disobedience, but an opportunity to be a co-regent or a co-creator with God. Our work or our creation is not *ex nihilo* like God's, but is a fashioning of new things out of already existing materials. In Genesis 3, after the Fall, there is a description of the development of the arts and sciences and of technological advance. Indeed, cultural development in general is brought into view here under the rubric of labor and marriage.

The creation of these things and values is for the glorification and service of Jesus Christ. Here Bonhoeffer argues analogically. Earthly things are an analogue of heavenly things albeit poor ones. For those who are open to it, glorious cultural development in the city of man gives a foretaste of the glory of the City of God. This analogous relationship includes production and commerce. In all of these things a world is coming into being that is waiting for its fulfillment in Christ. Sin, of course, casts its long shadow over us, in marriage and in labor. Sin makes us continually

---

[27] Bonhoeffer, *Ethics*, 205.

aware that we are no longer in Paradise, and it is true that some people experience their work as God's curse. Bonhoeffer comments on joyless work as he saw it on a visit to his friend, Jean Lasserre, in northern France.

> I have seldom felt so strongly that I was among those who labor and are heavy-laden as in the mining town in northern France where I have just been on holiday. It is a joyless, driven, humiliated, abused, and soiled existence, which is inherited and passed on from fathers to children and children's children. Wherever people experience their work as God's curse on humanity—there you will find those who labor and are heavy-laden.[28]

Since Christ's call is to all of us, we do not have to look only at hard, physical labor as the burden of life. "No, those who labor and are heavy-laden do not all look the way Rembrandt drew them in his 'Hundred Guilder' picture—poverty-stricken, miserable, sick, leprous, ragged, with worn, furrowed faces. They are also found concealed behind happy-looking, youthful faces and brilliantly successful lives."[29] In the shadow that the Fall casts over our work, Jesus lightens our load by showing us how better to carry it.

God's Commandments and Business Ethics

BONHOEFFER WAS looking for concreteness in his discussion of the commandment of God. In other words, how can God

---

[28] Bonhoeffer, *London*, 371.
[29] Ibid., 372.

instruct mankind if His speech is not clear? "God's commandment, revealed in Jesus Christ, is always concrete speech *to* somebody.... It is always an address, a claim, and it is so comprehensive and at the same time so definite that it leaves no freedom for interpretation or application, but only the freedom to obey or to disobey."[30]

There are parts of Scripture in which the words of God are clear, for instance, in the Ten Commandments. Other parts of Scripture are not so clear. The commandment of God not only forbids; it obligates. It not only restricts, it sets us free to live as authentic human beings. However, there is another dynamic element involved in the commandment of God. It is precisely the mandates themselves. Because the four mandates of marriage, labor, government and church have been given by God, these mandates carry the authority of God. Our everyday life within these mandates carries a certain divine stamp of approval. We can move away from the life of doubting our vocation in business to a joyful certainty of God's approval of that vocation. We no longer have to be second-class citizens in the Kingdom of God, but indeed children of God joyfully performing the will of God in business.

How is this possible? "If anyone is not willing to work, let him not eat."[31] "Let the thief no longer steal, but rather let him labor, doing honest work with his own hands, so that he may have something to share with anyone in need."[32] This is clear biblical instruction. These commands

---

[30] Bonhoeffer, *Ethics* 275.
[31] 2 Thessalonians 3:10.
[32] Ephesians 4:28.

are not only negative, as if our work life were a feverish attempt not to break the eighth commandment; "Thou shalt not steal" These commands are positive in that they encourage us to live joyfully within the will of God, in this case the world of work and business.

Bonhoeffer does not discuss the commandment of God from a natural law basis, that is, it does not spring from the created world. The commandment of God comes to us from above, and it gives us a warrant for ethical discourse. The authority to speak this commandment is given to labor, marriage, government and church. It is not given to church alone or to government alone. Each of these mandates interacts with the others in a relationship of complementarity and limitation. In this way the commandment of God becomes manifest.

For instance, under the mandate of labor, both Old Testament and New Testament teaching would be brought to bear upon our behavior in business and the labor force. The interactions of daily life as well as our obligations to marriage, government and church will inform us of the commandment of God which becomes an all-embracing unity.

Business ethics here cooperates with the other mandates as the commandment of God which operates at the center of our lives. This commandment gives fullness and wholeness to life. The complete expression of the commandment of God is revealed in Jesus Christ.

> The commandment of God becomes the element in which one lives without always being conscious of it, and, thus it implies freedom of movement and of action, freedom from

the fear of decision, freedom from fear to act, it implies certainty, quietude, confidence, balance and peace. I honour my parents, I am faithful in marriage, I respect the lives and property of others, not because at the frontiers of my life there is a threatening "thou shalt not," but because I accept as holy institutions of God these realities, parents, marriage, life and property, which confront me in the midst and in the fullness of life."[33]

The purpose of God's commandment is liberty. It is permission. Since we are discussing business here, we have a development of the commandment of God concerning business. Beginning with the creation accounts to "dress and keep the garden," the Ten Commandments of Exodus confront us with "Thou shalt not steal," and "Thou shalt not covet." The commandment continues through the Sermon on the Mount; "Give to those who ask you;" and the Pauline admonition "let him labor with his own hands." God is placing us within this world of work. King Solomon would counsel us that for some it is possible to take joy in work. This also is a gift from God. This whole development leads us to the mandate of labor. It is possible to take joy in our work, in our business endeavors because we are operating within the will of God.

This gives to us a certain surety and confidence in our work. There is a cooperation with God in what we are doing. Business ethics as such ceases to scrutinize every moment of the work day. It ceases to ask, "Are you making the best and highest use of your time in this activity?" The commandment of God in terms of labor allows a certain

---

[33] Bonhoeffer, *Ethics*, 276.

natural rhythm of the work day from clock-in, to the morning coffee break, to hard and frenetic activity, to lunch, to meetings, to the drive home. "The self-tormenting and hopeless question regarding the purity of one's motives, the suspicious observation of oneself, the glaring and fatiguing light of incessant consciousness, all these have nothing to do with the commandment of God, who grants liberty to live and to act."[34] Therefore, God desires freedom of action in the workday within the limits of His will.

The reality of God is the living reality. The revelation of God is the historical revelation of Jesus Christ, and the Holy Spirit brings this reality to us every day. Since God is good, the reality of living in Christ will place us in "the good". Good, here, is not a standard or a system, but a person.

Rather than opposing my life to a standard of good, it is Christ Himself who is my life. My life is not my work or my business or my family only, but Christ is my life. What message or purpose Christ may wish to reveal in my life may not be clear to me, but I can have peace and contentment today knowing that Christ is my life. Therefore, in a business context, my goal is that God will be known to be reality in me and through me. This, then, becomes the first principle of all business ethical reflection.

[34] Ibid., 279.

CHAPTER 3

DISCOURSE ON BUSINESS ETHICS

IN THE CORPUS of Dietrich Bonhoeffer's writings there is no specific section on business ethics. However, following the teaching on the mandate of labor, Bonhoeffer presents human labor as a part of discipleship. This is the correct way to think of our life in business. It is part of the way of discipleship that Christ has prepared for His followers. Ethical action is part of our everyday life in business. Labor also instructs us analogically. Human labor is a representation of spiritual labor. Christ labored and we labor. "God had himself endured toil and labour for man's sake (Isa. 43.24), and the soul of Jesus labored on the cross for our salvation even unto death (Isa. 53.11). The disciples are given a share in this work, in the proclamation, in the defeat of Satan, and in intercessory prayer."[1]

In his early discourses as a pastor in Barcelona, Bonhoeffer comments on ethics in general and on business in particular in one of his lectures to his congregation in 1929. In this early lecture, Bonhoeffer is already encouraging his hearers toward a life of dynamic discipleship. His ethical discussion is not an attempt to find the "universally valid", "...we do not intend to embark on the essentially hopeless attempt to present universally valid Christian norms and commandments applicable to contemporary ethical questions."[2] Pondering the universally valid would be similar to the captain of a sailing ship in a dead calm considering moving the rudder of the ship to the right or to the left. A moving ship, however, can be steered, and many times intuitive action must be taken immediately without a lot of pondering. "Only in the actual execution of a given action do the concepts of 'good' and 'bad' apply, that is, only in the given present moment; hence any attempt to explicate principles is like trying to draw a bird in flight."[3]

The disciple in business has tremendous freedom of action and also tremendous responsibility. The disciple of Christ is trying to put into practice the will of God. There are, no doubt, helps available, but the disciple is alone before God, responsible and free. Acting thus in freedom is

---

[1] Dietrich Bonhoeffer, *The Cost of Discipleship* (New York: Simon & Schuster, 1995), 209.

[2] Dietrich Bonhoeffer, *Barcelona, Berlin, New York, 1928-1931*, DBWE Vol. 10 (Minneapolis: Fortress Press, 2008), 360.

[3] Bonhoeffer, *Barcelona*, 360.

creative. God the Holy Spirit is personal and relates to us personally. He does not relate to us as a set of rules to be carefully figured out. The Holy Spirit brings before us God's love as revealed in Christ. This loving relationship also moves us toward action that will rightly display the love of God. The disciple's action in business is loving and free. These considerations have caused some to characterize Bonhoeffer as a "Christ mystic," and so he may be. "Christ-mysticism means that the Christian takes part in the life and death and resurrection of Christ....Christ-mysticism does not, therefore, mean to discover a Christ in the depth of one's soul. It means participation in the reality of the Christ who encounters me and takes me in tow, incorporating me into his reality."[4]

The world exists for Christ, and Bonhoeffer wanted to participate in the life of the world as the place of living Christ-mysticism. So, in his writings there is not an inordinate emphasis on other-worldliness or upon this-worldliness, but on reality. In the sufferings that we may encounter in the world of business, we may encounter also the sufferings of Christ. This kind of Christ-mysticism does not fly off into total subjectivism. There is a place in our discipleship for the clear speech of God, or a place for the concrete commandment, and so *Ethics* teaches. Our discipleship in business, then, includes the clear speech of God in the vagaries of the moment in which things may not

---

[4] Georg Huntemann, *Dietrich Bonhoeffer: An Evangelical Reassessment* (Grand Rapids, Michigan: Baker Book House, 1993), 114-115.

be clear. We are learning Christ mystically through this process.

There are clear words of God for us as Bonhoeffer illustrates in *The Cost of Discipleship*. In his treatment of the Sermon on the Mount these clear words are brought out under chapter headings such as: The Brother, The Woman, Truthfulness, Revenge, The Enemy—the "extraordinary." In the chapter on revenge, Bonhoeffer states, "By willing endurance we cause suffering to pass. Evil becomes a spent force when we put up no resistance. By refusing to pay back the enemy in his own coin, and by preferring to suffer without resistance, the Christian exhibits the sinfulness of contumely and insult."[5] This is a comment on Matthew 5:39, "Do not resist the one who is evil. But if anyone slaps you on the right cheek, turn to him the other also." We might differ from Bonhoeffer's application of this passage, or possibly his exposition of its meaning. However, if we agree, then this teaching of Christ becomes applicable to our journey in business. For example, the CEO of a corporation who is also a disciple of Christ finds his business decisions informed by this teaching of Christ as well as other teaching.

I am not free to repay the evil doer in his own coin. In not resisting evil against me, I am exposing it. I am exhibiting it for what it is, and I am pulling its sting. This teaching is clear enough although difficult to do. However, there is another side of the coin which is the deliberate resisting of evil when appropriate. The possible methods of resistance would be in view here also. The company employee might humbly discuss with his superior some

---

[5] Bonhoeffer, *Discipleship*, 142.

subtle racial discrimination that exists in the firm. The disciple might call attention to a relaxing of accounting standards. This is the disciple's journey—to perform these right actions at the appropriate times. Even clear teaching cannot provide the exact formula by which to gauge all of our actions.

Bonhoeffer discusses the business climate of the day as one in which smaller business entities are ruined by larger ones. No doubt, since business is composed of human beings we can expect sharp practice, cutting corners, and other subterfuge to be part of the business scene. He comments here:

> ...if we are to participate in economic life, are [we] compelled to be part of all this [?] Can a Christian responsibly be a business-person in this sense? We often hear of a double morality, one for personal life and one for business. But this assertion is obviously impossible because we have but one conscience, which we must obey in all situations. The question is merely whether with this one conscience we can also be business people.[6]

It is true, as the discussion in Chapter Two proceeded, that the conscience might masquerade as the voice of God while insinuating the voice of the devil. Perhaps more to the point here would be the Apostle's injunction that "whatever does not proceed from faith is sin,"[7] or the Apostle James' instruction against double-mindedness.

Should we stay in a business vocation even though there is a strong pull to live a double morality? Should we

---

[6] Bonhoeffer, *Barcelona*, 374.
[7] Romans 14:23.

61

persevere in this rugged path of discipleship? The answer is yes. "We are living in a strange world, and yet we do want to be Christians. Fleeing that world does not help; the only thing that helps is entering this complicated reality fully conscious and fully trusting that, as long as we abide with God, he will also guide us through this world."[8]

Others are depending on us for their welfare. We are doing good to family and neighbors. Engaging in business is not a choice between good and evil. We are choosing the good through working and earning, but our path in business may be tortuous and problematic. Responsible action before God may require us to do things that are misunderstood or perhaps to take harsh actions. Fleeing the business world does not help. Responsible discipleship leads us into the complicated reality of business. "Precisely here, too, we end up in distressing situations that require the ever-renewed relationship with the divine will."[9] Our personal walk with Christ is our only hope of negotiating this winding path.

The disciple in business needs God's grace that comes to him new every morning. Like the prophet Jeremiah who looks out over the destruction of Jerusalem, the business person may look out over a business ruin or an ethical ruin and know that it is by God's mercy and grace only that perseverance is possible. As Jeremiah looked out over a ruined and destroyed Jerusalem he said, "The steadfast love of the Lord never ceases; his mercies never come to an end; they are new every morning; great is your faithfulness."[10]

---

[8] Bonhoeffer, *Barcelona*, 375.
[9] Ibid., 375.
[10] Lamentations 3:22.

Business ethics as a branch of ethics has a warrant to speak as a part of the general discourse on ethics. However, this discourse does not have the nature of timeless and placeless discussion. The weight of business-ethical decision making is felt as I am in the midst of a business-ethical dilemma or problem, or I find myself under the necessity of taking action. As the actor portraying Christ in the passion play at Oberramergau, Bavaria, said, "If I did not feel the weight of His cross, I could not play the part."

In his book *Ethics*, Bonhoeffer discusses the desirability of bringing young people into the discussion with those more ethically mature, with experience in the trials of business. These are the people who bring the proper weight or *gravitas* with them. These are people from whom we can learn. I may arrive at the right answer to a business ethical problem, but the person who has lived through the experience has more authority in speaking the same answer.[11] This weighty ethical discussion will get us beyond the usual ethical case of "it goes without saying." Ethics rises to the top as a theme when the moral "self-evident" course has not been followed or when the course is not clear. Business ethics is more than a theme; it is real life. "That convulsive clinging to the ethical theme, which takes the form of a moralization of life, arises from fear of the fullness of everyday life; it is a flight into a position which lies outside real life...."[12] So business ethics in Bonhoeffer's sense is not pointing fingers or rehearsing the coincidence of

---

[11] Dietrich Bonhoeffer, *Ethics* (New York: Touchstone, 1995), 266-267.

[12] Bonhoeffer, *Ethics*, 263-264.

bad actions that caused some catastrophe. It is seeking to do the will of God and to portray the character of Christ in all one's vocation.

In the previous chapter, we mentioned the four mandates of labor, marriage, government, and church that Bonhoeffer presents in order to think about the commandment of God in each area. As mentioned, Bonhoeffer does not discuss this commandment of God on a natural law basis. It does not spring from the created world, but it comes to us from above. The authority to speak this commandment of God is given to marriage, labor, government, and church, not to church alone or to government alone. There is an interaction between the courses of action required in each of these areas of life so that, indeed, we see that we are living one life and indeed, living the commandment of God. This could be an example of Karl Barth's and Bonhoeffer's "dialectical theology," which means in this case that these different areas of life interact and speak with authority and thus produce the right decision in business. All areas of life impinge with their own authority into the decision of the moment.

It is easy to see how the mandate of marriage could inform a business decision. I am committed to my wife and I must love her "as Christ loves the Church." It is possible to put in a fifteen-hour day in business. However, if my business pattern revolves around the fifteen-hour day from which my marriage is suffering, the commandment of God with respect to marriage begins to inform me that some changes need to be made in my work life for the sake of my marriage and family. We could multiply examples of this type.

In a reciprocal way, business ethics [operating in the mandate of labor] cooperates with the other mandates as the commandment of God which operates at the center of our lives. This commandment gives fullness and wholeness to life, not division and strife. The complete expression of the commandment of God is revealed in Jesus Christ.

Personal Formation as Business Ethics

IT IS LIFE in the workplace that provides the opportunity for the Christian to be conformed into the image of Christ in exactly that business context. Since much of my time is spent in the business organization, the formation of Christ in me must take place through my participation in business. Here, my action in business reveals and forms my ethics and becomes part of my formation for Christ or against Him. This may sound like the wrong way to discuss ethics. In this case we are emphasizing human action forming ethics. However, the disciple in business has no all-encompassing standard to impose on her fellow-workers. She may not have an all-encompassing standard to impose upon herself. "...Christ's disciples have no rights of their own or standards of right and wrong which they could enforce with other people; they have received nothing but Christ's fellowship. Therefore the disciple is not to sit in judgment over his fellow-man because he would wrongly usurp the jurisdiction."[13] My "judgment" extends only as far as my

---

[13] Bonhoeffer, *Discipleship*, 185.

authority in the business. I may be entrusted to make decisions of various types with respect to matériel or my fellow workers. Any spoken or insinuated "judgment" of persons beyond my authority is office gossip, rumor, officiousness, slander, or character assassination.

Formation takes us into the mystery of Christ and the mystery of other people. There is more involved in this formation than business calculations of less and more. Formation as business ethics takes me into the secret springs of human action. The disciples in business thusly formed will "…not hold themselves aloof from the processes of life as spectators, critics and judges; [but will] share in life not out of motive of 'shall' and 'should,' but from the full abundance of vital motives, from the natural and the organic, and from free acceptance and will, not in humourless hostility towards every vital force and towards every weakness and disorder."[14] Simply to operate on the level of profit calculation is to miss the path of discipleship and the meaning of my actions.

> However, to live without mystery means not to know anything about the secrets of our own lives or those of other people, or of the world's secrets. It means passing by that which is hidden within ourselves, other people, and the world, staying on the surface, taking the world seriously only to the extent to which it can be calculated and exploited, never looking for what is behind the world of calculation and of gain.[15]

---

[14] Bonhoeffer, *Ethics*, 265.
[15] Bonhoeffer, *London*, 360.

Perhaps it might be hopeful and truthful to say that Christian business ethics is designed to serve the proclamation and formation of Christ in us. The church is back in the world on Monday morning striving with all other workers, entrepreneurs and managers for the accomplishment of definite tasks and the success of the business enterprise. The formation of Christ in us occurs as we are conformed to His death and resurrection. Therefore, in my journey in business, no task is too small or too large for me to do. With a good will I set my hand to the task before me, not trying to distinguish myself as being greater or lesser, but carrying in my body both the dying and living of Christ.

Business Ethics as Formation

BONHOEFFER IS NOT an idealist. He is interested in discussing the concrete ethical action. So, in that tradition, business ethics seeks to help the follower of Christ in the day-to-day life in business. For Bonhoeffer the Christian understanding of the person at the most basic level is always that of the person in a social and ethical encounter with the other person; this is the Christian basic-relation of I and You, self and other. It presupposes the theological axiom that the human person always exists in relation to an Other, namely God, and that human relations are in some way analogies of this fundamental relation.[16] Since human beings are created in the image of God, all the people with whom I come into contact have a claim upon me. They may be part of the body of Christ, or they may be "enemies" for whom I must show love according to the teaching of Christ.

The claim of the 'other' upon me is a claim to treat that person with dignity, honesty, love and fair dealing and to treat the other as a bearer of the image of God and a brother of Christ. The claim of the other rests in God and God's work. My development also depends upon all these "others" with whom I interact. The individual, then, exists in relation to an 'other.' To be individual does not mean to be solitary, but 'others' must necessarily be there.[17]

Life in the business world develops character--for better or for worse. There is no exercising or controlling my will without the give and take of daily life. When we encounter other people, we encounter human beings with ideas, wills and abilities. In business competition or cooperation, we are placed in social situations in which we must make decisions and act. Our motives may be clear or not. All of this social 'dialectic' forms character. Through this interaction the business and the business person will be formed and shaped. Good businesses use ideas to improve performance. Indeed, our job may be to provide new ideas for experimentation and implementation in the business enterprise. However, Christ has another purpose for us in the business context. "It is not Christian men who shape the world with their ideas,

---

[16] Dietrich Bonhoeffer, *Sanctorum Communio*, DBWE Vol. 1 (Minneapolis, MN: Fortress Press, 1998), 50.

[17] Bonhoeffer, *Sanctorum Communio*, 51.

but it is Christ who shapes men in conformity with Himself."[18]

The road of ethical decision-making and wisdom in business is our road of discipleship. We are at liberty now to work in business and to act. Our lack of clarity in ethical decisions should not make us despair or cause us to seek escape from the arena of business action. "The real man is at liberty to be his Creator's creature. To be conformed with the Incarnate is to have the right to be the man one really is. Now there is no more pretence, no more hypocrisy or self-violence, no more compulsion to be something other, better and more ideal than what one is. God loves the real man. God became a real man."[19] It is for this reason that we can be real men and women, and act with confidence.

In speaking of business ethics as formation, we are asking the question, "How does Jesus Christ take form in our world?" Business provides the context for most of us. Business ethics as decision and action gets beyond theorizing and speculation. We will be formed as a result of our decisions and actions. Happily for us, there is a concrete place upon which we can stand. "Ethics as formation is possible only upon the foundation of the form of Jesus Christ which is present in His Church. The Church is the place where Jesus Christ's taking form is proclaimed and accomplished. It is the proclamation and this event that Christian ethics is designed to serve."[20] It is to the Church

---

[18] Bonhoeffer, *Ethics*, 82.
[19] Ibid., 82.
[20] Ibid., 89.

that we now turn for a discussion of its role in the form of Christ and Christ's formation in us.

The Church and Formation

IT IS IMPORTANT that Christ's death and resurrection be lived by us in business. This is where the preaching and teaching of Christ breaks out of the assembly and into the world. This involves the business person in displaying charity, integrity, mercy, and a loving spirit that may involve reproving and receiving correction. Therefore, the life and formation of the Christian in community is important here for our experience of love, fellowship, and teaching. It is important that businesspersons enjoy the same love and fellowship that others find in the community. We need community--real community and interaction--not just church attendance, in order to stimulate the creation of wisdom.[21] It is from the entire church community, from zealous youth to wise elders that a cohesive spirit of wisdom may be cultivated. The road of wisdom is also the road of discipleship.

We may fail in business decisions or in our job. We may do wrong things with full knowledge of what we are doing. However, it is Christ who takes our guilt of bad business practices and makes it His own thereby freeing us from the burden. But like Christ's word to the woman taken in adultery, his word to the disciple in business is, "go and sin

---

[21] D.J. Moberg, "Practical Wisdom and Business Ethics," *Business Ethics Quarterly*, 17 (3) 2007, 545-546.

no more." And so the church also bears the businessman's guilt and suffers with him---not condemning, because he also is part of the body. The church is also guilty of apostasy from Christ; so we confess and experience forgiveness together. The Church confesses herself guilty of not loving the businessperson and helping her to pursue Christlike character. [22]

In many of his writings Bonhoeffer uses the word *Gemeinde*, which is usually translated as "church-community." Christ exists as church-community [*Gemeinde*]. The Apostle Paul is continually making this point. Where the body of Christ is, there Christ truly is. Christ is in the church-community, as the church-community is in Christ (1 Cor. 1:30, 3:16, 2 Cor. 6:16; Col. 2:17, 3:11). "To be in Christ is synonymous with 'to be in the church-community'". [23] The church-community is part of our life in Christ. "The Church is nothing but a section of humanity in which Christ has really taken form....In the first instance, therefore, she has essentially nothing whatever to do with the so-called religious functions of man, but with the whole man in his existence in the world with all its implications. What matters in the Church is not religion but the form of Christ, and its taking form amidst a band of men." [24]

Our bodily fellowship with Christ now is found in the church-community. We are baptized into this body, and the bodily fellowship of Christ is continually ministered to us

---

[22] Bonhoeffer, *Ethics*, 112.
[23] Bonhoeffer, *Sanctorum Communio*, 140.
[24] Bonhoeffer, *Ethics*, 85.

71

through the Word, baptism and Lord's Supper. The new humanity is the Church, and the church-community is open to all who desire the presence of Christ. Remember the Church is not an institution, but persons. "Since the ascension, Christ's place on earth has been taken by his Body, the Church. The Church is the real presence of Christ." [25] The Church, then, is not religion; it is community.

The people who make up the church-community have various jobs and posts in business, in education, or in government. The Church is concerned with the lives of all of its members as they represent Christ in business or in some other vocation. In the church-community men and women continue to receive revelation. Revelation exists in the church with the church being thought of not as an institution but as persons. [26] The disciples need revelation. They need to hear from God. Scripture is of foremost importance here. However, Bonhoeffer was opposed to the "positivism of revelation." By this he meant the religious guise in which Christianity was presented. It means a pre-formed, ready-made answer from the Bible (or more likely from religion) to all of the disciple's problems or questions. It is a traditional or pietistic answer that can lead to mental and spiritual laziness. This "positivism of revelation" could lead to a religious cliché substituting for real help. For instance, the business person might receive an exhortation from the church "to do the right thing," but this may be

---

[25] Bonhoeffer, *Discipleship*, 241.

[26] Dietrich Bonhoeffer, *Act and Being*, DBWE Vol. 2 (Minneapolis: Fortress Press), 105.

unhelpful in the particular situation in which she finds herself.

Revelation comes in the church-community through hearing the Word preached, through the Sacraments, and from loving interaction with fellow believers as well as Scripture reading. Bonhoeffer liked to call this the secret discipline or *arcanum disciplinum* of the church. The members of the church-community grow stronger through hearing the word concerning Christ—it produces faith. They are also strengthened through participating in baptism and the Lord's Supper. This provides real spiritual food and real spiritual strengthening. This discipline is unknown by the world. It is practiced by the church-community in secret.

During Bonhoeffer's life the Protestant Church was suffering blow after blow in Germany from both external and internal foes. Today, the role of traditional Protestantism appears to be even more at the margins of European culture. This line of thought leads to some of Bonhoeffer's last writings in *Letters and Papers from Prison* concerning "religionless Christianity." He saw religion as a historical form of Christianity that was passing away. He speculated on what it would mean to be a "secular Christian." However, in that situation the "secret discipline" [*arcanum disciplinum*] would be of great importance.[27] So by implication would be the church-community. What form this church-community would assume is not clear, but the disciples need for each other would remain.

---

[27] Dietrich Bonhoeffer, *Letters and Papers from Prison* (Touchstone, New York: 1997), 280-281.

As Eberhard Bethge mentions, the phrase "secret discipline" occurs only twice in *Letters and Papers from Prison*. This does not mean that the idea had not been important for many years in Bonhoeffer's thinking. Although the secret discipline assumed further aspects, the original meaning as understood and practiced by the Finkenwalde students is reported by Bethge as:

> ...the early Christian practice of excluding the uninitiated, the unbaptized catechumens, from the second part of the liturgy in which the communion was celebrated and the Nicene Creed sung. This was the origin of the "arcane discipline." As students in Finkenwalde, we were surprised when Bonhoeffer sought to revive this piece of early church history of which we had never taken any notice."[28]

In the dark days of the Church struggle, Bonhoeffer wrote to his friend, Erwin Sutz about the importance of the church-community in educating and forming its own pastors in discipleship. No doubt, Bonhoeffer was seeing the infiltration of Nazi statist values in the university and seminary as well.

> I no longer believe in the university; in fact I never really have believed in it—to your chagrin! The next generation of pastors, these days, ought to be trained entirely in church-monastic schools, where the pure doctrine, the Sermon on the Mount, and worship are taken seriously—which for all three of these things is simply not the case at the university and under the present circumstances is impossible. It is also time for a final break with our theologically grounded reserve about whatever is being done by the state—which

---

[28] Bethge, 881.

really only comes down to fear. 'Speak out for those who cannot speak'—who in the church today still remembers that this is the very least the Bible asks of us in such times as these?[29]

Faith is also maintained and encouraged in the church-community. Bonhoeffer teaches that faith is something dynamic. It has to be won or experienced over and over again. This dynamism does not negate God's predestination of His people nor human will in pursuing a continuing justification. The resolution of these two [predestination and free will] is to be found in the church. God elected the church and each one in it. We find our true life and calling in the church, in fellowship with others. My brothers and sisters bring Christ to me, and I bring Christ to them. Our actions are mutually supportive and mutually revelatory. The truth of God's word is revealed to me in them and through them; so that the Church becomes the locus of God's continuing activity and the reality of God's continuing revelation.

This is not necessarily the modern "Openness of God" theology in which God progresses and grows with His people. Bonhoeffer doesn't disavow God's sovereignty. He writes in a disapproving way concerning the pragmatism that he encountered among American theologians concerning this 'growing God.'

> ...the active God must first be confirmed by the 'usefulness' of his activity with regard to human beings in order to be true, and second, insofar as God enters to such an extent

---

[29] Bonhoeffer, *London*, 217.

into his own activity that it is only within that very activity
that he actually grows. Union Theological Seminary and the
realm of enlightened Americans have greeted and parroted
with extraordinary liveliness [William] James's thesis of the
'growing God.' This thesis combines religion and faith in
progress in a virtuoso manner, so that the one finds its
support and justification through the other.[30]

On the contrary, he teaches the attributes of God in such
a way as to make them more dynamic for us and as actually
coming into our purview. All this takes place in the church-
community. The disciple then on the basis of his life
together with the body of Christ, becomes a little reflection
of the Body of Christ in the world, or in the vocation to
which God has assigned him. The dynamism of God in the
Church works out also individually in the home and the
work place so that the presence of Christ is really there in
the world. Now, this presence of Christ may be little-noticed
by those outside the church. Those whom God has chosen
out of the world must also be given the gift of faith and then
their eyes will be opened to the wonder of Christ in the
world and in the Church. They will be made aware that they
are new beings and that they were created for this. They bear
the new humanity while they themselves are borne in all
their actions by the community of faith, by Christ.[31] "Faith,
then is brought to life in the community and through the
community. For only in the community, am I embraced as
individual and as humanity in existentiality and in
continuity—of course, precisely 'in faith' that, however,

---

[30] Bonhoeffer, *Barcelona*, 311.
[31] Bonhoeffer, *Act and Being*, 119-120.

knows itself to be possible at all in the power of the community of faith, in which faith is brought to life."[32] Bonhoeffer's point, clearly, is that faith exists, or flourishes best, in community.

So the Church is the form that Christ is taking in the world. Christ is truly present in the church-community through preaching and the administering of the sacraments. "...Jesus Christ is not dead, but alive and speaking to us today through the testimony of the Scriptures....If we would hear his call to follow, we must listen where he is to be found, that is, in the Church through the ministry of Word and Sacrament."[33]

The church-community through its ministry is the focal point for the disciples through the Word of God and the body and blood of Christ by which the members are nourished and strengthened. The Church is concerned with Christ being incarnated in every member. So our walk in the world is very important. Without this practical context for discipleship, a walk with Christ is only theoretical. Christ is for me and the church-community is for me, and my vocation in the world is for my good and the good of the world. The world is not changed by programs of the church. The member of the church-community lives in this world. However, Christ being formed in me and displayed in me, as my vocation leads me through the business world, allows the Church's prophetic voice to be heard precisely in the middle of the world.

---

[32] Bonhoeffer, *Act and Being*, 121.
[33] Bonhoeffer, *Discipleship*, 225-226.

The Church and Business

THE WORLD HAS a prince, and it is the devil. There is a distinction between the kingdom of God and the kingdom of the world. Business is the outstanding representative of the kingdom of the world. That is why Bonhoeffer uses the word "assault" when he discusses the Christian's relation to the world. The Christian remains in business not because of his responsibility for the course of the world, but for the sake of Christ and His Church. This is the disciple's assault on the world—an assault in humility and meekness, in not pressing his claim to be the foremost, in considering others as better than himself. This assault has more effectiveness if we are members of the church-community. In that way the difference between the church-community and the world is illustrated more clearly.

We die to the world, yet live in it. Therefore, Christian spirituality is lived and refined in the secular calling. We live in the world as people who really exhibit the character of Christ. That is the way that we die to the world, not by going out of it. This is the real assault on the world. "The value of the secular calling for the Christian is that it provides an opportunity of living the Christian life with the support of God's grace, and of engaging more vigorously in the assault on the world and everything that it stands for."[34]

The disciple in business finds a natural and normal movement between worship in the church-community and work in the enterprise. This movement and relationship informs us of the reality of the church which is

---

[34] Bonhoeffer, *Discipleship*, 265.

"...understood not in moments of spiritual exaltation, but within the routine and pains of daily life, and within the context of ordinary worship."[35] This relationship does not express itself in senseless hostility toward business, or as Bonhoeffer put it in *Sanctorum Communio*, toward culture. The disciples do not place their trust in culture. Bonhoeffer saw the tension between culture and the church-community as increasing not softening. The same would be true for the tension between the *sanctorum communio* [communion of saints] and business, so that, the communion of saints can never be fully absorbed by business or the surrounding culture. However, these two things, church and culture, are not total opposites either.

Bonhoeffer here is following the lead of Martin Luther in discussing the relation of Christ and culture as one of paradox. As mentioned earlier, the world of business provides a context for us to live out the Christ-life. At the same time, the world of business is riddled with sin and sinful practices. Each year we hear of new scandals as thousands of employees suffer the effects of poor decisions that coworkers and managers have made. God sustains this world for the benefit of the human race and the benefit of His Church. For the disciple in business, then, "...(he) knows that he belongs to that culture and cannot get out of it, that God indeed sustains him in it and by it; for if God in His grace did not sustain the world in its sin it would not exist for a moment."[36]

---

[35] Bonhoeffer, *Sanctorum Communio*, 281.
[36] H. Richard Niebuhr, *Christ and Culture* (New York: Harper Torchbooks, 1975), 156.

Business, then, is our place of spiritual warfare and living the Christ-life. The Church encourages us and sustains us in this. Indeed the preaching and teaching of the Church along with its Sacraments prepare and empower us for this. Bonhoeffer mentions that Luther's return to the world from the monastery did not involve a more positive attitude on Luther's part toward the world. His was a protest against the secularization of Christianity in the monasteries, and his "return from the cloister to the world was the worst blow the world had suffered since the days of early Christianity."[37] "[Luther's] call to men to return to the world was essentially a call to enter the visible Church of the incarnate Lord."[38]

The Church nourishes the body of Christ for its weekly assault on the world. This assault is a spiritual assault which is manifested in real actions of love. Christ's command to love others as He has loved us makes all the more dramatic the difference between the kingdom of the world of business and the Kingdom of God. "Love for our neighbor is our will to embrace God's will for the other person; God's will for the other person is defined for us in the unrestricted command to surrender our self-centered will to our neighbor, which neither means to love the other instead of God, nor to love God in the other, but to put the other in our own place and to love the neighbor instead of ourselves;…This attitude, however, is not within our means, but is 'poured out by the Holy Spirit into our hearts.'"[39]

---

[37] Bonhoeffer, *Discipleship*, 48.
[38] Ibid., 265.
[39] Bonhoeffer, *Sanctorum Communio*, 171.

God's grace and love gives the disciple a certain business-ethical orientation. The love of Christ will show us actions in business to do and actions to avoid. This business ethics of the love of Christ places a certain limit on our relationship with business. Our membership in the church-community also places a limit on us. A clash may occur when the claims of business and the church-community conflict. This may not be a public *cause célèbre*, but the clash may occur in a hidden and private way when a member of the church-community knows that she has come to a line that she cannot cross. "We shall at once know when the limit has been reached, for every member of the Church will then be obliged to make a public confession of Christ, and the world will be forced to react, either by calculated restraint or open violence. Now the Christian must suffer openly."[40] When one suffers the whole body suffers. The confession of Christ by one member encourages the confession of Christ by all the members. The individual and the church-community suffer. Now the church-community enters into the suffering of its Lord. So the Church and the business world interact; each informing the other. The loving action of the disciple in business illustrates the character of Christ and becomes the ethics in business of the church-community.

This interaction between the church-community and business is necessary and established by Christian teaching. The path of discipleship leads us into a process of becoming. The bar of discipleship was set very high for us many years ago by St. Ignatius in the early second century. As he was

---

[40] Bonhoeffer, *Discipleship*, 266.

traveling from Antioch to Rome to be put to death, he wrote seven letters to various churches. In the letters to the Church in Ephesus and to the Church in Rome he uses the identical phrase, "Now am I beginning to be a disciple."[41] This was said on his journey to being fed to the lions in the amphitheater in Rome for refusing to offer prescribed sacrifices to the gods. There is a new beginning and a becoming to the discipleship of Ignatius even as he approached the end of his life through martyrdom. Becoming is always the *motif* of discipleship. Bonhoeffer is following Luther here who emphasized that Christians prove their identity not in what they have become, but always through the process of becoming.

Jesus Christ gives us the world as the sphere of reality in which to operate. Our vocational responsibility is a limited one, but in the decision-making required of us the life of Christ becomes a reality in us. This is not a theoretical exercise, but real action according to the will of God. This is not abstract ethics nor an elegant system which proves to be unexceptional for all time. "... Christ is not a principle in accordance with which the whole world must be shaped."[42] Christ is a real man and wants us to be real and authentic human beings before God. Christ is not a philosopher like Kant trying to discover if "the maxim of my action can become a principle of universal legislation." The greater question is, "whether my action is at this moment helping my neighbor to become a man before God."[43] Indeed, this is

---

[41] J.B. Lightfoot, *The Apostolic Fathers* (Grand Rapids, Michigan: Baker Book House, 1978), 64, 77.

[42] Bonhoeffer, *Ethics*, 86.

[43] Ibid., 86.

the path of business ethics for the disciple. Our good will and the consequences of our actions are both important in our task. Therefore, this ethic takes us beyond the teachings of both Jeremy Bentham and Immanuel Kant—two of the ethical beacons in the business school.

CHAPTER 4

BEYOND BENTHAM AND KANT

A UNIVERSITY COURSE in business ethics would include a variety of ethical approaches including egoism, virtue ethics, utilitarianism, the ethics of Immanuel Kant, the libertarian ethics of Robert Nozick, the development of property rights from John Locke, the difference principle of John Rawls, the ethics of care, and the human rights approach. This is valuable information. It allows us to interact with different ways of decision-making in business ethics questions. All of these ethical approaches have something to commend them. For instance, virtue ethics has a wonderful sound to it. It seems like an approach that would be highly desirable, and so it is. Virtue ethics does not replace other ethical approaches but complements them. Business ethicist, Manuel Velasquez, defines virtue ethics in terms of moral action. "An action is morally right if in carrying out the action the agent exercises, exhibits, or develops a morally virtuous character, and it is morally wrong to the extent that by carrying out the action the agent exercises, exhibits, or develops a morally vicious character."[1]

In all these ethical approaches there is an ethical case that runs the system aground. Some hypothetical or actual ethics case can be presented which is difficult to resolve because of conflicting duties, virtues, etc. Even virtue ethics must steer between excess and deficiency of the virtue lest ethical sloth or fanaticism be produced. In these ethical approaches a fundamental division of ethical systems has developed between consequentialist and non-consequentialist ethics. In consequentialism the actor is concerned about the future likely consequences of any action that he makes. On this basis decisions are made. Egoism is a type of consequentialist ethic. Egoist ethics looks at how the consequences of any ethical move will affect him. This is the main ethical consideration. How the consequences of actions factor into the egoist's view of the good is not clear. The egoist might hold any view of what constitutes the good. So we might hold with more or less approbation the egoist's decision depending on what is our view of the good.

A non-consequentialist position would be any ethical view that operates from principle, that is, there are certain principles of good action that should always be done. The businessperson operating from principle will always do certain actions and avoid others because those actions conform to fixed ethical principles. An example of non-consequentialist ethics is the system of Immanuel Kant.

---

[1] Manuel G. Velasquez, *Business Ethics* 4th ed. (Upper Saddle River, New Jersey: Prentice Hall, 1998), 137.

There are certain actions that conform to principle and they must be done without exception.

Bentham

THE GREAT REPRESENTATIVE of consequentialism is Jeremy Bentham who founded a school known as the "philosophical radicals." That is, they believed that they had gotten to the root of the problem of all ethical decision-making, particularly political decision-making. Bentham's work was an analysis of penal law and law reform, and his school is known as utilitarianism. Bentham was aided in the development and propagation of utilitarianism by the philosopher and economist, James Mill, the father of the renowned John Stuart Mill who in his early days was also a proponent of utilitarianism.

But apart from the special conditions of the 1820's, utilitarianism, as it came to be called, was a far more vulnerable doctrine than Benthamism. It was no longer a set of principles for legal and constitutional reform, but had been elevated by James Mill to a philosophy....Yet when he converted utilitarianism into a complete philosophy, every principle he stated was taken to be not merely a guide to social action or legal reform, but a moral principle.[2]

This ethical approach has had great influence in American politics and in schools of business. A shorthand

---

[2] Shirley Robin Letwin, *The Pursuit of Certainty* (Indianapolis, Indiana: Liberty Fund, 1998), 231-232.

motto for utilitarianism is "the greatest good for the greatest number." The moral decision is found by adding up the positive utilities and subtracting the negative utilities. If there is a net addition to overall utility, the action should be done. If there is a net diminution of social utility, the action should not be done. Bentham further developed this moral arithmetic through the felicific calculus which is described in his famous book, *An Introduction to the Principles of Morals and Legislation*.

Bentham was a prolific writer on social and political questions. He wrote the panopticon papers in which he laid out a scheme for prisons. This was his most sustained attempt to show the virtues of a rational solution for prison reform based on a simple change in architecture. In 1784 Bentham announced to Parliament that, "he had a method that made it possible to become master of all that might happen to a certain number of men, to dispose of everything around them so as to produce on them the desired impression, and allow nothing to escape, nor to oppose the desired effect."[3] The guard station was to be in the middle of a circular prison with the cells arranged around it in circular fashion. This would allow the guard to continuously observe the prisoners and make sure that they were busy at their tasks of work or self-improvement. Some nursing stations in hospitals today are arranged in this panopticon fashion.

His famous book, *Principles of Morals*, became well-read by heads of state in Europe. In it he claimed to have solved the principle of legislation which was through the

---

[3] Letwin, 191.

calculation of utilities. Bentham wanted a surer way to decide on legislation rather than oratory and passionate discourse by gentlemen politicians. "…utility could give the clue to distinguishing good from bad without useless disputes about words. It rested every case on a 'matter of fact; that is future fact—the probability of certain future contingencies,' so that debates about politics and legislation could be settled by judgment, not passion, by bringing evidence of 'such past matters of fact as appear to be analogous to those contingent future ones.'"[4]

This calculation was made possible through Bentham's development of the felicific calculus. This was basically a pleasure-pain score sheet, and this is where the radical nature of Bentham's philosophy comes in. Good is pleasure. Evil is pain—nothing more and nothing less.

"Nature has placed mankind under the governance of two sovereign masters, *pain* and *pleasure*. It is for them alone to point out what we ought to do, as well as to determine what we shall do. On the one hand the standard of right and wrong, on the other the chain of causes and effects, are fastened to their throne."[5] The felicific calculus was a complex list of scoring pleasures and pains according to intensity, duration, certainty, proximity and other categories. The principle is simple. Add up the pleasures and pains and the course of action is clear. If the sum of the pleasures is greater than the sum of the pains, the action in question should be done. This will operate at the individual

---

[4] Ibid., 132.
[5] Jeremy Bentham, *An Introduction to the Principles of Morals and Legislation*, ed. By W. Harrison (Oxford: The Clarendon Press, 1948), 126.

level and at the level of larger bodies such as corporations or the state. If this sounds like a maximization of utility exercise in microeconomics, that is correct. The idea of consumer utility and indifference curves derives from the work of Bentham. The expected consequences of actions as they produce utilities is the touchstone of this ethical system.

Kant

IMMANUEL KANT IS the great representative of non-consequentialism. His is a principle-based ethic and truly one of the great achievements of Western philosophy and ethics. Kant explains his system in the *Foundations of the Metaphysics of Morals.* Kant began his search for a "pure moral philosophy completely cleansed of anything empirical." In other words he is not going to consider the results of ethical action. Results can be good or ill. There is no guarantee as to the results of our actions.

Human reason alone is the means by which the principles of justice can be approached. Kant envisioned a system of laws to which all members of society could consent, and which would be consonant with the maximum extension of freedom to the citizens. It is to human reason that we must appeal for the validation of what Kant called the "Universal Principle of Justice." This appeal is an appeal to the principle of non-contradiction. If there are laws [generally speaking] to which everyone does not consent then the result will be civil chaos. Therefore, the laws should produce peace and universal consent on the basis of reason.[6] Every person, then, possesses dignity and moral authority on the basis of reason alone.

While respect is due because of the existence of reason in the human being, good character may not necessarily follow. A person must not only know the right thing but must also do the right thing, and this doing must come from the motive of fulfilling one's duty. Goodness of moral character then depends on a person's intentions or good will. Nothing is good except a good will which manifests itself in intention to always do one's duty. In other words, my motive for action is good. I desire to act in accordance with my duty. This good motive gives my action moral worth.[7]

The person of good will has a certain internal law-giving ability which informs our duty. A person of good moral character acts from duty. But, what is our duty? If we can find our duty we will find an obligation which directs us absolutely or categorically. This is the wording which Kant used for his famous ethical principle. He named it the categorical imperative. This principle gives us our duty; it is imperative, and it admits of no exceptions.

Kant states the Categorical Imperative in three formulations. The Formula of Autonomy states, "I ought never to act in such a way that I could not also will that my maxim should be a universal law." The Formula of Respect for the Dignity of Persons states, "Act so that you treat

---

[6] Roger J. Sullivan, *An Introduction to Kant's Ethics* (Cambridge: Cambridge University Press, 1997), 13.

[7] William H. Shaw and Vincent Barry, *Moral Issues in Business*, 10th ed. (Belmont, CA: Thomson Wadsworth, 2007), 61.

humanity, whether in your own person or in that of any other, always as an end and never as a means only." The Formula of Legislation for a Moral Community states, "All maxims that proceed from our own making of law ought to harmonize with a possible kingdom of ends as a kingdom of nature."[8]

The first and second formulations are the most well-known. To be a solid principle of duty, it must be the case that the principle of my action can be made into a universal law. Likewise, duty requires that I treat other persons as ends in themselves. This forms the rock of moral principle in Kant's system. This is the Categorical Imperative. It admits of no exceptions. To act on the Categorical Imperative requires the development of maxims—short sayings that describe appropriate moral action. Morally good intention, then, is to always act on those moral maxims that are consistent with the Categorical Imperative. These maxims are tested logically, not empirically.

As an illustration of the Categorical Imperative, Kant discusses the case of lying promises. That is, when would it be morally legitimate to make a lying promise, or more generally, when would it be morally legitimate to lie? The analysis begins with a situation in which there is some advantage to me from making a lying promise. I make a promise which I know I will not keep. However, to be effective, I assume that my acquaintance will believe my promise. Is this a morally legitimate action? No, it is not, because if we could make this maxim of behavior into a universal law; the making of promises itself would cease.

---

[8] Sullivan, 29.

They would not be believed. Contract-making, for instance, depends on promise keeping between buyer and seller without which much societal interaction would cease. This, however, is an empirical consequence. Kant's system does not depend on this, but on the logical contradiction involved in making a lying promise. Therefore, lying or making lying promises is wrong without exception.

The prohibition against lying is of much greater antiquity than Kant. One of the Ten Commandments of Exodus likewise prohibits it. So this would seem to imply even more strongly that telling lies is wrong without exception. However, the Bible itself reports what seems to be commendable lying in the case of the two Hebrew midwives, Shiphrah and Puah who allowed the Hebrew male children to live rather than put them to death as the king of Egypt had commanded. Their response to the king seems to be a stretch of the truth at least, "...the Hebrew women are not like the Egyptian women, for they are vigorous and give birth before the midwife comes to them."[9]

So in these two approaches, one from Bentham and one from Kant, we have both a calculation of consequences and a non-consequentialist approach. Ethical decision-making, however, is not so easily divided into these categories, but may be a blend of these and other approaches. As mentioned above, there are several ways of thinking about ethical decision-making. I find that I have used several of these methods in making ethical decisions in my life which doesn't justify either the decisions or the methods of arriving at them.

---

[9] Exodus 1:19.

BONHOEFFER AND BUSINESS ETHICS

In analyzing the problem in a consequentialist/non-consequentialist way, we are engaging in abstraction and tearing apart the unity between the good and the real, the man and his work.[10] The person and the work go together. We can never go far enough to know the depths of our motives or the far-reaching consequences of our actions. We don't have that kind of wisdom or psychological depth. "Therefore, do not pronounce judgment before the time, before the Lord comes, who will bring to light the things now hidden in darkness and will disclose the purposes of the heart. Then each one will receive his commendation from God."[11]

Beyond Bentham and Kant

BONHOEFFER'S DISCUSSION of ethics goes beyond Bentham and Kant. The inward journey can never plum the depths or springs of wrong motive. In other words, in seeking for Kant's good will [that is, totally good will without alloy] the person will not find a will that is crystal pure, one without the slightest hint of self-seeking or pride. The outward journey cannot see far enough to know the ultimate outcome of any ethical move. The future is not knowable to us.

---

[10] Dietrich Bonhoeffer, *Ethics* (New York: Touchstone, 1995), 189.

[11] 1 Corinthians 4:5.

94

An ethic of motives or of mental attitudes is as superficial as an ethic of practical consequences. For what right have we to stop short at the immediate motive and to regard this as the ultimate ethical phenomenon, refusing to take into account the fact that a 'good' motive may spring from a very dark background of human consciousness and unconsciousness and that a 'good attitude' may often be the source of the worst of actions? And just as the question of the motivation of action is in the end lost in the inextricable complexities of the past, so, too, does the question of its consequences finally disappear from view in the mists of the future. [12]

Bonhoeffer is arguing for an approach to ethics that deals with human beings as real people in relation with a real God who is the good Creator of the good creation. He is not developing some ideal standard with which to compare all motives and consequences. "In principle neither of these has anything to commend it in preference to the other, for in both of these the question of good is posed in abstract terms and in isolation from reality....Good is reality itself, reality seen and recognized in God."[13] Our motives are many and varied. Our actions affect not only us but our community. To discuss motives and consequences as a continually morose judge of human nature is to treat persons as divided beings, but persons were created as whole and indivisible. Our origin is in creation and our goal is the kingdom of God. We are in the midst of this reality of God and the world. We know this reality to be true because of the Incarnation. It is in the person of Jesus Christ that our

---

[12] Bonhoeffer, *Ethics*, 190.
[13] Ibid., 190.

inquiry concerning good becomes participation in the Good—in the reality of God and the world. [14] For Bonhoeffer the journey inward became a means for travelling the journey outward in a more Christ-like fashion. "The real focus of Discipleship, however, is neither the interior of man nor the exterior of the world, but the person of Jesus Christ, His image and example." [15]

Our discipleship walk, then, is a walk with a person not with a set of principles. In this walk with a person we relate to reality as it is involved with God and the world simultaneously. In his book, *The Philosophy of Tolkien: The Worldview Behind The Lord of the Rings*, Philosopher Peter Kreeft states this same conclusion in a different way.

> Duty is really to persons, not to principles....Like Eowyn, Frodo has been 'commanded', by a person, not a principle. And he knows and trusts his commanders (Elrond and Gandalf) and therefore obeys them. He does not say, as Kant did, that he obeys reason, or duty, or the Categorical Imperative. He does not say, 'I think my rational duty is this, and I obey it.' Ultimately, obedience and duty come down to knowing, trusting, and loving a person. [16]

Kreeft also steers away from utilitarianism because it is simply an excuse for doing bad things. We find moral virtue exemplified through charity, self-forgetfulness, and self-

---

[14] Ibid., 190-193.

[15] Sabine Dramm, *Dietrich Bonhoeffer, an Introduction to His Thought*, tr. By Thomas Rice (Peabody, MA: Hendrickson Publishers, Inc., 2007), 83.

[16] Peter J. Kreeft, *The Philosophy of Tolkien: The Worldview Behind The Lord of the Rings* (San Francisco, CA: Ignatius Press, 2005), 196.

sacrifice, not through utilitarianism. [17] We are now away from elaborately constructed ethical systems. Therefore Bonhoeffer states, "It is not by astuteness, by knowing the tricks, but only by simple steadfastness in the truth of God, by training the eye upon this truth until it is simple and wise, that there comes the experience and the knowledge of the ethical reality." [18]

However, there are clear, Scriptural precepts by which we are to walk. There is clear speech of God in the Law and in the teaching. Therefore, action is the only possible attitude towards the Law. [19] We are now on the razor's edge of life. On the one side is the free walk with Christ. On the other is the clear speech of God in Scripture. It is here that we need to understand more clearly what Bonhoeffer is saying. He would like to live a life of joyous, freedom before God. The disciple's action would have to be free because of the gift of grace. God has already opened the way to man through the Incarnation, therefore, no system of working back toward God can be permitted. No system of rules whereby the disciple can gain more grace exists.

This ongoing relationship to God's will is the great moral renewal Jesus brought about, the dismissal of principles, of fundamental rules—in biblical terms, the law. And precisely this dismissal is a consequence of the Christian idea of God. For if there were indeed a universally valid moral law, following it would involve taking the path from human beings to God. If I have principles, I feel I am secured *sub specie aeternitatis*. In that case, I would control my own

---

[17] Kreeft, 196.
[18] Bonhoeffer, *Ethics*, 67.
[19] Ibid., 48.

relationship with God, as it were, and there could be ethical action without any immediate relationship with God. But the most important aspect is that I would then become a slave to my principles and would be surrendering the most precious human possession, my freedom. When Jesus places people immediately under God, new and afresh at each moment, he restores to humanity the immense gift that it had lost, freedom.[20]

This freedom of action that God gives to human beings is creative in the ethical realm and in the realm of the spirit. A dull repetition of the Law is uncreative and leads toward a type of slavery to the Law. As Bonhoeffer puts it, the disciple stands before God and the world without any backing. We must bear the entire responsibility for our use of the creative freedom that God gives us. The freedom of the disciple is, paradoxically, bound up with the commandment of God— the clear speech of God.

God's commandment is fully revealed in the life of Jesus Christ. It not only forbids; it liberates. For instance, consider God's commandments not to steal, to work with our own hands, and Christ's statement that "My Father is working until now, and I am working."[21] In my work life I am not simply trying to avoid the prohibition of stealing, but I have a positive example in Christ. I may be following Christ by analogy in my work. In other words, I have permission to work, to do a good job, and to take pleasure in it. I am liberated in that way. The joy of human work does

---

[20] Dietrich Bonhoeffer, *Barcelona, Berlin, New York 1928-1931*, DBW Vol. 10 (Minneapolis: Fortress Press, 2008), 365.
[21] John 5:17.

not violate the commandment of God. In fact, it precisely fulfills it.

The commandment of God impinges upon, that is, liberates me in all areas of life. It is a unity. It operates at the center of life not just on the frontiers. With this opening understanding of the commandment of God as revealed in Jesus Christ, the disciple begins to act with more confidence and more sureness. Action and decision-making become not so much of a burden because of the command and the liberty that comes from God. This is different from the simply "ethical." Bonhoeffer has some good sentences on the moroseness of the "ethical."

> In all circumstances the 'ethical' demands clarity, directness, purity and consciousness in human motives and deeds....The commandment of God permits man to be man before God....It lets man eat, drink, sleep, work, rest and play.....It does not continually ask him whether he has some more urgent duties. It does not make man a critic and judge of himself and of his deed, but it allows him to live and to act with certainty and with confidence in the guidance of the divine commandment. The self-tormenting and hopeless question regarding the purity of one's motives, the suspicious observation of oneself,...,all these have nothing to do with the commandment of God,...The permission to live, which is granted in the commandment of God, takes account of the fact that the roots of human life and action lie in darkness and that activity and passivity, the conscious and the unconscious are inextricably interwoven.[22]

---

[22] Bonhoeffer, *Ethics*, 278-279.

In business, therefore, my concern is with doing the will of Christ. The will of Christ may be to humbly confront my boss about wrong action, or to quietly go about the task at hand.

Christ becomes more and more the center of the disciple's life in business. As Bonhoeffer's work moved into the 1940's through his time in prison, he wrote more on Christ's lordship being exercised through powerlessness and weakness. "...this Lord exercises his lordship always and solely through powerlessness, service, and the cross. But this lordship is undoubted. Bonhoeffer is not defending a lost lordship and certainly not any lost positions. Indeed, he wants to give up 'positions' in order that he can learn to understand anew how the suffering and powerless Christ becomes the defining, liberating, and creative center of this world."[23]

This is a business-ethical way that is certainly far beyond Bentham and Kant. It seems that God is giving the business person or employee a path of knowing Christ, and that path leads straight through business. The life of work in business is the path of sanctification. It is the path of, shall we say, mystical union with Christ? What other path could there be other than the path of my vocation? The following of Christ through business becomes more and more a path of not defending my position, not being a tyrant and leading through weakness. The picture outlined here and the possibilities are mind-boggling. Sabine Dramm comments on this point in Bonhoeffer.

---

[23] Eberhard Bethge, *Dietrich Bonhoeffer: A Biography*, (Minneapolis, MN: Fortress Press, 2000), 864.

Although Bonhoeffer does not speak of becoming one with Christ or of a mystical union as such, his statement that the image of the believer and disciple must be identical with that of Christ is reminiscent of the witness borne by those who have experienced *unio mystica*, that is, the mystical union—or at least a form of mystical experience—linked with the figure of Christ....Those who have testified about their mystical experiences speak remarkably often about stations and stages in their experience of God, and of visitations by God. In connection with the image of Christ, Bonhoeffer says that 'the splendor of Jesus Christ will shine through us while we are still on this earth'; there is a 'progression from awareness to awareness, from clarity to clarity, and on to ever more perfect identity with the image of the Son of God.' He calls this process the 'indwelling of Jesus Christ in our hearts': 'The life of Jesus Christ has not yet come to an end on this earth. Christ lives on in the lives of his followers....He who became man, was crucified and transfigured, enters into me and lives my life.'[24]

The experiences of business which further illuminate the reality of Christ in our hearts do not necessarily bear the businessperson upward into the music of the spheres, "but downward into the hard realities of this world, a world in which God wishes to play a role. For Bonhoeffer as well, and in particular, the immediate experience of Christ bears completely concrete consequences for man."[25]The small and large decisions of daily life in business provide the real stuff of our discipleship—the concrete situation. God speaks to us through this. "God alone is concrete...the concrete situation is the substance within which the Word of God speaks; it is

---

[24] Dramm, 87-88.
[25] Dramm, 88.

the object, not the subject, of concretion."[26] The Holy Spirit continues to teach us through these business decisions. "The Holy Spirit is found only in the present, in ethical decision, not in fixed moral regulations or in an ethical principle."[27]

Again in a lecture to his congregation in Barcelona entitled "Basic Questions of a Christian Ethic," Bonhoeffer drives home the point that we are in action and the Holy Spirit is in action with us. "The letter kills, but the Spirit gives life, as Paul put it in a familiar passage, meaning that the Spirit is found only in the execution of actions, in the present; a fixed Spirit is no Spirit at all. Hence ethics is found only in the execution of a deed, not in the letter, that is, in the law."[28]

Individual or Social Ethics

FROM WHAT HAS BEEN said earlier about Bonhoeffer's approach to ethics, we should suspect that to make a division between individual and social ethics would run the risk of dividing the person into unrealistic spheres. Bonhoeffer stated the question this way, "Instead, it is a question—to be precise—of whether in the realm of Christian ethics it is possible to make statements about worldly orders and conditions, thus, e.g., about state, economy, science, i.e., whether Christian ethics has an

---

[26] Bethge, 443.
[27] Bonhoeffer, *Barcelona*, 368.
[28] Ibid., 368.

interest in worldly orders and conditions, or whether these things of the world are in fact 'ethically neutral,' i.e., do not fall 'in the realm governed by ethical imperatives.'"[29]

The answer is, of course, that larger matters are a concern of Christian ethics.

> Because all created things exist for the sake of Christ and on the strength of Christ, they therefore stand under the commandment and claim of Christ. For the sake of Christ and on the strength of Christ there exist and should exist worldly order in state, family, economy. For the sake of Christ the worldly order stands under the commandment of God. Here one should note that this is not a matter of a 'Christian state' or 'Christian economy,' but rather of the just state, the just economy as a worldly order for the sake of Christ. Thus there is a Christian responsibility for the worldly orders, and there are assertions within a Christian ethic that refer to this responsibility.[30]

We are one whole person, and the ethical decision should be in keeping with the integrity of the person. From the example of Bonhoeffer's life, it is clear that he was involved in larger church questions and larger societal questions. Our discipleship may lead to involvement with larger and larger numbers of people or be related to only a few. In a personal letter to his brother, Karl-Friedrich, Dietrich states, "Things do exist that are worth standing up for without compromise. To me it seems that peace and social justice are such things,

---

[29] Dietrich Bonhoeffer, *Conspiracy and Imprisonment 1940-1945*, DBWE Vol. 16 (Minneapolis: Fortress Press, 2006), 541.
[30] Bonhoeffer, *Conspiracy*, 543.

as is Christ himself."[31] However, peace and social justice must have a concrete context in which the individual may work. God is concrete and He speaks to us in the concrete situation.

The primary concrete situation for the disciple is the church-community. It is there that he finds that his actions are not entirely his own. There are community claims upon him and individual actions affect the larger community. From the church-community, the word of God is proclaimed, not only for the community itself, but for the whole world. In this way the disciple and the church-community are involved with larger and larger circles of people. The church-community will act differently and make its proclamation of the dominion of Christ over all things including the political and economic realms in different ways depending on its situation. The mission-church is different from the church that is recognized by the state which is different from the church under persecution. Individual action and action by the church-community require wisdom depending upon which situation the church-community finds itself.

Bonhoeffer had an interest in large social questions, for instance, the peace movement. So he addressed the Ecumenical Council of Christian Churches in Fanø, Denmark in 1934,

> Peace on earth is not a problem, but a commandment given at Christ's coming. There are two ways of reacting to this commandment from God: the unconditional, blind

---

[31] Dietrich Bonhoeffer, *London, 1933-1935*, DBWE Vol. 13 (Minneapolis: Fortress Press, 2007), 285.

obedience of action, or the hypocritical question of the Serpent: 'Yea, hath God said…? There shall be peace because for the Church of Christ, for the sake of which the world exists. And this Church of Christ lives at one and the same time in all peoples, yet beyond all boundaries, whether national, political, social, or racial.[32]

This was Bonhoeffer's ethical position which had national and international import. However, to simply make pronouncements takes the ethical into the realm of the theoretical or the ethereal only. The concrete point of action for him was his refusal to take up arms in the event of his draft into the German army. This was a costly and dangerous decision. One could be shot in Germany at that time for such a stance. "On the shore of the Danish island of Fanø Bonhoeffer was asked by a Swedish participant, 'What would you do in a war, Pastor?' It is said that Bonhoeffer let a handful of sand run out through his fingers and then looked quietly at his questioner: 'I pray that God will give me the strength not to take up arms.'"[33]

Bonhoeffer's concrete decision in the concrete situation had further consequences that shaped the course of his life. His brother-in-law Hans von Dohnanyi got him a job with the *Abwehr*, the German Office of Military Intelligence, which saved him from the draft and placed him in contact with anti-Hitler conspirators. One decision leads to the next. We do not know how the future course of events will run. We must act in faith and as Christ's followers.

---

[32] Bonhoeffer, *London*, 307-308.
[33] Eberhard Bethge, Renate Bethge, and Christian Gremmels, *Dietrich Bonhoeffer: A Life in Pictures* (London: SCM Press, 1986), 133.

Individual ethical decision and social ethical decision must complement each other. There is no necessary opposition between the two. Christ loves the world. He loves the Church. He loves the individual. Our action is not divided. Our action is moving all the while under Christ's love.

CHAPTER 5

BUSINESS
AS A MANDATE OF GOD

"TO SPEAK OF THE world without speaking of Christ is empty and abstract....It is God's will that there shall be labour, marriage, government and church in the world; and it is His will that all these, each in its own way, shall be through Christ, directed towards Christ, and in Christ....This means that there can be no retreating from a 'secular' into a 'spiritual' sphere."[1]

Based on our discussion in Chapter 2, we have seen that Bonhoeffer places human labor under the creation mandates. We are now thinking about labor in the world under the heading of business or commerce. Labor is one of the four mandates which God graciously gives to humankind for our

---

[1] Dietrich Bonhoeffer, *Ethics* (New York: Touchstone, 1995), 204.

preservation. These are areas in which we may be heartily involved for our own occupation and for the glory of God. Bonhoeffer defines work as "the creative service of God and Christ toward the world and of human beings toward God."[2] In this section I would like to discuss the whole area of business and commerce as the manifestation of this mandate of labor. God's grace is manifested to us in the mandates. God continues to preserve the world and the human race after its calamitous fall into sin. The preservation of life and human action within life can be death-dealing or life-affirming. God in a certain sense affirms man as he is—fallen—with a view toward the new creation. "God's new action towards man is that he preserves him in his fallen world, in his fallen orders, on the way to death, approaching the resurrection, the new creation, on the way to Christ."[3]

God preserves the world for His good purposes. Business organization and action is the way that earning a livelihood is made possible in our era. Markets continue to develop making business cooperation possible on a world-wide scale. This is the way the world-system is developing, and God preserves us in it and through it. To view business activity with contempt is to disparage the gift of labor which God gives to us at creation.

The mandate of labor brings human work into being and by extension, commerce. This does not mean, however,

---

[2] Dietrich Bonhoeffer, *Conspiracy and Imprisonment: 1940 – 1945*, DBWE Vol. 16 (Minneapolis, MN: Fortress Press, 2006), 550.
[3] Dietrich Bonhoeffer, *Creation and Fall, Temptation* (New York: Macmillan, 1953), 88.

that all businesses and commercial endeavors enjoy a fixed status and blessing similar to a divine right. "The consequence of all this [the divine mandates] can all too easily be the assumption of a divine sanction for all existing orders and institutions in general and a romantic conservatism which is entirely at variance with the Christian doctrine of the four divine mandates." [4] The world of business and commerce is not exempt from criticism or reform or reorganization. The divine mandate of labor is fully revealed to us in the one commandment of God as it is revealed in Jesus Christ. Labor, business and commerce are not exempt from the proclamation of the church, but they may be called back to the fulfillment of the divine mandate out of which they operate. Employer and employee in view of the incarnation of God are called upon to live as men and women before God which means to live not for oneself but for God and for others. [5]

Georg Huntemann summarizes Bonhoeffer's work about God's preservation of us through labor and business and the proclamation of the church concerning labor and business.

In Bonhoeffer's lectures on Genesis, which were published later under the title Creation and Fall, it becomes clear that for Bonhoeffer creation is a fallen creation. Creation is partially undone by the power of evil and will not be fully restored and liberated until the second coming of Christ. Until then, it is the preservational ordinances that keep this creation from being destroyed by the chaotic powers of evil. Preservational ordinances are a defense against the power of

---

[4] Bonhoeffer, Ethics, 283.

[5] Ibid., 292.

evil. But Bonhoeffer also knew that any human, secular, or social order could be and had to be shattered "when it closes up within itself, hardens and no longer permits the proclamation of revelation."[6]

"Shattering of secular and social orders" might be a job for a professional revolutionary. Bonhoeffer was not that. However, unusual times may call forth unusual responses. In his own life the first open opposition to established institutions was in his support of the Confessing Church against the state-sponsored Protestant Church of the so-called "German Christians." In this, Dietrich was accompanied by Martin Niemöller and others. The next opposition was a clandestine one demonstrated by his participation in the conspiracy against Hitler. It is also true that when institutions close themselves to the revelation of God, they may self-destruct or atrophy.

The mandate of labor operates with its own authority. The Church operates with its own authority. Simply because the Church has the commandment of God as revealed in Jesus Christ does not mean that the Church has any role in dominating labor or government or family. The Church proclaims Jesus as Lord over all the earth. Christ's lordship frees all the mandates to realize their essential character and to relate in a fruitful way with each other.[7] The mandates allow the Church to minister to its members and non-members without overreaching its proper bounds.

---

[6] Georg Huntemann, *Dietrich Bonhoeffer: An Evangelical Reassessment* (Grand Rapids, MI: Baker Books, 1993), 236.

[7] Bonhoeffer, *Ethics*, 293-294.

The church-community which comes into being around the word of God is not meant to dominate the world, but to proclaim that the Word of God rules the entire world. In its humility then the church-community relates to business in weakness which illustrates what Bonhoeffer would call the weakness of the word. "God lets himself be pushed out of the world on to the cross."[8] The existence of the church-community is a reminder of this fact.

It is evident that the business community and the church-community operate with different objectives in mind. Businesses are human organizations that exist for the achievement of definite goals such as the production of high-quality goods and services, the realization of profits, and efficiency in production. This is understandable and obviously commended by God under the rubric of the labor mandate. Societies in general are organized around the achievement of a definite goal or purpose.

Societies are found in the "world." Communities are also found there, but the most typical form of community in Bonhoeffer's work is the church-community. This community is characterized by meaning or representative action or self-representation. In primitive religious communities, cultic activity before a deity is often almost pure self-representation.[9] The church-community represents itself before God through word and sacrament, and God is represented before the community through word and sacrament. Societies (business organizations) and

---

[8] Dietrich Bonhoeffer, *Letters and Papers from Prison* (New York: Simon & Schuster, 1997), 360.

[9] Dietrich Bonhoeffer, *Sanctorum Communio*, DBWE Vol. 1 (Minneapolis, MN: Fortress Press, 1998), 104.

communities (the church-community) operate differently with different mandates under the approbation of God. Businesses exist in order to produce goods and services, while the church-community joyfully affirms its own existence week-by-week.

Business as Preparing the Way

IN MEDITATING ON the fullness of life and the multi-dimensionality of life, Bonhoeffer wrote to Eberhard Bethge that it is really faith that makes this possible. However, perhaps there are some things that can be done to prepare the way for the reception of faith. "We have to get people out of their one-track minds; that is a kind of 'preparation' for faith, or something that makes faith possible, although really it's only faith itself that can make possible a multi-dimensional life, ..."[10]

Our minds can fixate on various things. In order to prepare for faith, we need some respite from the matters that so occupy us. I may worry greatly about where I shall obtain my next meal. Perhaps my worry is with layoffs or finding a good job. I need liberation from these outward worries before inward liberation can take place.[11] This outward liberation may, indeed, prepare me for the reception of faith. It is here that business can help in preparing the way through job creation through business expansion and the

---

[10] Bonhoeffer, *Letters*, 311.
[11] Ibid., 9.

practice of giving. Many businesses do this. This is simply an example of what it means to prepare the way.

> For him who is cast into utter shame, desolation, poverty and helplessness, it is difficult to have faith in the justice and goodness of God….To allow the hungry man to remain hungry would be blasphemy against God and one's neighbor, for what is nearest to God is precisely the need of one's neighbor….If the hungry man does not attain to faith, then the guilt falls on those who refused him bread. To provide the hungry man with bread is to prepare the way for the coming of grace.[12]

In this quote from *Ethics* we find the famous implicit question, "Who is my neighbor?" The answer has already been given in the parable of the Good Samaritan. We see our neighbor as the person in need that is before us. It is then that love for my neighbor will be demonstrated through action. Some businesses are involved in meeting the needs of neighbors. Those needs could be multiform such as, the need for bread, justice, fellowship, discipline, and freedom. Business may be able to help in preparing the way for the reception of faith by our neighbors.

To operate in this way business cannot be a programme designed to prepare the way, but the business activity itself must be a spiritual reality, i.e., the businessperson must be living the vocation given to him by Christ and incarnating Christ in the vocation. The vocation itself is not Christ nor is the businessperson Christ. But the context of business provides the continuing path of discipleship and preparing the way in humility. For this reason employers and

---

[12] Bonhoeffer, *Ethics*, 135-136.

employees should never see each other or customers as machines or as objects. "But wherever man becomes a thing, a merchandise, a machine....the reception of Christ is impeded."[13] Our treatment of fellow workers in the business may help prepare the way for the reception of faith in them. As business people, we need to have care with business jargon which may depersonalize potential customers or others with whom we might have dealings.

The church also has a responsibility to inquire into the functioning of whole economic systems, and how those systems might prepare the way for faith or hinder its reception. There might be an inquiry into the systems of capitalism, socialism, and various types of collectivism in terms of preparing the way. The church might be able to point out certain events or practices that are hindering the reception of faith. However, to make a positive contribution here, the church needs the advice of experts in political economy. Hence, there is a doctrinal work and a technical political-economic work that can proceed from the church. There is a word of doctrine and a word from Christian life that combine for good counsel to the state and business.[14]

In a long letter to Eberhard Bethge in *Letters and Papers from Prison*, Dietrich muses on the joys of friendship and of freedom to pursue activities like art, learning, music, and play. These things are not directly included in any of the four mandates but certainly make for a happier and more pleasurable human existence. Business might prepare the

---

[13] Ibid., 138.
[14] Dietrich Bonhoeffer, *Ethics*, DBWE Vol. 6 (Minneapolis, MN: Fortress Press, 2005), 361-362.

way for these other good things of life and also might broaden the exercise of freedom in these areas. Some businesses are involved in these things through support for the arts and support for education. Stability of income and employment also allows the work force to pursue these things.

> Marriage, work, state, and church all have their definite, divine mandate; but what about culture and education? I don't think they can just be classified under work,...Who is there, for instance, in our times, who can devote himself with an easy mind to music, friendship, games, or happiness? Surely not the 'ethical' man, but only the Christian. Just because friendship belongs to this sphere of freedom ('of the Christian man'?!), it must be confidently defended against all the disapproving frowns of 'ethical' existences, though without claiming for it the *necessitas* of a divine decree, but only the *necessitas* of *freedom*.[15]

Business can help us to live a more humane existence, perhaps to enjoy ourselves. Businesses can help in human flourishing, and the overcoming of some of the grimmer realities of life such as poverty, hunger, sickness. This is a way that God ministers grace to us, (common grace) and through this a preparing of the way for faith could happen.

Business as Part of the Natural World

IN DISCUSSING THE natural world, Bonhoeffer rightly accuses Protestant thought of leaving the discussion mainly

---

[15] Bonhoeffer, *Letters*, 192-193.

in the hands of Catholic theologians and ethicists. Since the time of Thomas Aquinas and before, Catholic theology has used natural law to illustrate God's grace so that the natural continues to have theological relevance. Protestant theology has seen nature as sunk so deeply in sin that relative differences between good and evil or between different kinds of evil were seen as not worth discussing. Grace here is all important. The loss is that we are left on the playing field of the natural without clear direction or guidance. To remedy this, Bonhoeffer introduced the categories of the ultimate and the penultimate. The ultimate word of God is the last word, the word of eschatology, the establishment of God's kingdom at the end of the age. The penultimate word of God concerns life here and now, discipleship, following Christ. The natural world has its proper place as part of the penultimate. The natural is not simply an area with which neither God nor man is concerned. There are tasks that are proper to us in the natural world.

Since we live in this natural world, Bonhoeffer took up the theme of "true worldliness." Labor is part of humankind's life in the world. It is part of our natural life. The modern development of labor is in business and commerce. To work here is truly to be a part of the world. The rule of Christ as proclaimed by the church does not subjugate or enslave business, but liberates business for genuine worldliness. "For the worldly orders...the dominion of Christ and the Decalogue do not mean in the first place the conversion of the statesman, the businessman, or the abolition of state harshness and gracelessness in favor of a falsely understood attempt to Christianize the state that itself wants to be a kind of church."[16]

The dominion of Christ is taken seriously when business is liberated to do what is proper to it, namely to produce and sell goods and services. The church-community proclaims the teaching of Christ and in doing so liberates business to pursue its true vocation. If the worldly orders will give space for the proclamation of Christ they will find their mandates and their genuine worldliness to be grounded in Christ.[17] This is possible because the teaching of both the Old Testament and the New enjoin upon us participation in marriage, labor, and government.

From the Old Testament accounts Bonhoeffer differentiates between creation and nature. Creation comes from God's direct action, nature or the natural is what we know after the Fall. Within the natural world there is a difference between the natural and the unnatural. The natural is directed toward the coming of Jesus Christ. The unnatural closes itself off from the coming of Jesus Christ.[18] For example, government may give space to the church-community for the proclamation of the Lordship of Christ. In that way government is open to the coming of Christ without being specifically Christian. However, government may persecute the church-community and in that way acts unnaturally in closing itself off from the coming of Christ. In the Incarnation God places his stamp of approval upon natural life whether in marriage, labor, or government.

---

[16] Bonhoeffer, *Conspiracy*, 548.
[17] Ibid., 549.
[18] Bonhoeffer, *Ethics* DBWE, 173.

A joyless and humorless cynicism toward the world is not Bonhoeffer's idea of an authentic discipleship of Christ. Part of the blessing of God upon us comes to us through natural life. Natural life, however, is not full knowledge of Christ nor our eternal destination. Therefore, we "do not love the world." [19] For the blessings we are grateful, "I think we honour God more if we gratefully accept the life that he gives us with all its blessings, loving it and drinking it to the full, and also grieving deeply and sincerely when we have impaired or wasted any of the good things of life..." [20] It is in the natural world that our whole field of activity is before us, and it exists for us. Bonheoffer encouraged his congregation in Barcelona in this way that we can engage in our work with a good will and a joyful heart. "The Christian's field of activity is the world. It is here that Christians are to become engaged, are to work and be active, here that they are to do the will of God; and for that reason, Christians are not resigned pessimists, but are those who while admittedly not expecting much from the world are for that very reason already joyous and cheerful in the world, for that world is the seedbed of eternity." [21]

At the same time we know that the earth—nature is under the curse of God. It is not as productive as it once was. We eat our bread, then, in the sweat of our face. There is sorrow involved in natural life. There is sorrow involved in business. "Thus the fruits of the field become both the bread which we eat with tears and the bread of charity, of

---

[19] 1 John 2:15.
[20] Bonhoeffer, *Letters*, 191-192.
[21] Dietrich Bonhoeffer, *Barcelona, Berlin, New York, 1928-1931*, DBWE Vol. 10 (Minneapolis: Fortress Press, 2008), 521.

him who sustains us...."[22] This is our world. This is nature. This is the knowledge of good and evil that has led to a life of division. Bonhoeffer repeats the Hebrew words *tob* and *ra* to make this point.

> This is the changed, the destroyed, world. At odds with God, with the other person and with nature, man cannot live, yet in this division of *tob* (good) and *ra* (evil), he cannot live without God, without the other person, or without nature. In truth he lives in the world of the curse, but just because it is God's curse that burdens it, this world is not totally forsaken by God; it is the world of the preservation of life, blessed in God's curse, pacified in enmity, pain and work.[23]

Businesspersons and Institutions

IN THINKING FURTHER about the mandates of labor, marriage, government and church, it is clear that all of these develop institutional forms. Labor has developed huge syndicates and unions, business has developed the huge corporate form. Marriage can develop a certain "normal" way in which the sanction of state and church authority can be applied. Divorce also has a certain institutional path which must be sought. The Church and Government both develop bureaucratically, and government, particularly has a tendency toward giantism. These institutions form part of the world system. They have legitimacy under the mandates

---

[22] Bonhoeffer, *Creation and Fall*, 85.
[23] Ibid., 85.

of God and preserve humankind against chaos. It is the preservation of humankind that is in focus. These institutions exist for our benefit. Everything in this "world" is for us.

In his visits to Confessing Churches in Prussia in 1940, Dietrich wrote a Bible study on this idea taken from the Apostle Paul, "all [things] are yours."[24] This was during the years of the church struggle which was against the infiltration of national socialist doctrine into the Church bureaucracy. The church-community is the gathering of the faithful. The Church contains the people—the church-community. Therefore, Dietrich writes on the basis of the Apostle's words,

> A tremendous promise for our church-communities that are so constrained, afflicted, tyrannized, and muzzled; our view becomes quite encompassing. All fetters that the world wants to impose on the church-community and its work are burst as if they were not there at all; the prison doors swing open, the great church bureaucracy collapses like a house of cards. The church-community is freed. *All things are yours.* The entire world belongs to you and must serve you.[25]

So the disciple in business or government or the Church can be at ease about performing the will of God. All of these things serve us in preservation, and they serve us because we are in Christ. The entire world and all bureaucracies, then, serve the church-community which is people gathered formally or informally for the worship of Christ.

---

[24] 1 Corinthians 3:22.
[25] Bonhoeffer, *Conspiracy*, 482.

120

Many members of the church-community live out their discipleship in business. How do the institutions of government and Church look from the perspective of business? Businesspeople are very good at project-planning and problem-solving in general. For many of them, problem-solving is part of their gifting and training. Which problems should the business enterprise solve? Certainly many suggestions could be made. Some businesses have provided counselors for their workforce in an attempt to solve the problem of divorce and other family or psychological problems among their workers. This seems to be a good idea and a good work, but this is not the primary area of business problem-solving.

Businesses concentrate on planning and problem-solving that are connected with their primary tasks of innovation, production, sales, cost-reduction and realization of profits. Other problems may be addressed by businesses, but these primary areas of activity allow business to fulfill the mandate of labor that comes from the creation accounts. If business does not concentrate on these things it will shortly not be a going enterprise, and workers will become unemployed thus negating the creation mandate of labor for the workforce. Businesses are not necessarily cold and calculating. It would be better to say that they are focused on their main problems. Rightly so, how else can they fulfill the mandate of labor?

The disciple of Christ works in this business environment. She is also a member of the church-community which preaches a message of God's love for the world. It is through her that the church-community witnesses to the world of business concerning its faith in Christ and seeks to make room for the gospel in the world.[26] This is the point at which each disciple's gifting and opportunities come into play on behalf of the gospel. The disciple relates to her business by living both law and gospel—that is, right action, as revealed in the Decalogue and justification of the sinner as revealed in the gospel.

The business community from its perspective can view the Church with approbation. Members of the church-community are working with a good attitude, they are doing right action, perhaps wise action, and they are living as justified sinners. Notice that these disciples are not living as persons whose sins have been justified, but as justified sinners. Workers from the church-community proclaim solidarity with all human beings as sinners and point to Christ as the great justifier. There is no flaunting of sin or pride in status as a justified sinner. In other words there can develop a mutual respect between the institutions of business and the Church as each performs the tasks appropriate to it under the mandates of God.

In his book *Cost of Discipleship*, Bonhoeffer further develops the theme of the relationship of the disciple and the world which consists of institutions like business and government. Since Christ is the mediator between God and man, He is the center and demands our allegiance in all things. "He is the Mediator, not only between God and man, but between man and man, between man and reality....Since his coming man has no immediate relationship of his own any more to anything, neither to

---

[26] Bonhoeffer, *Ethics* DBWE, 357.

God nor to the world; Christ wants to be the mediator."[27] Therefore there can be no direct allegiance to business. As in all areas of life Christ stands between us and an immediate relationship with other things. This is, no doubt, a hard teaching—a hard reality—that confronts Christians in the world. An immediate relationship means a direct relationship. We, of course, do have relationships with people and groups and institutions, but in all these relationships Christ is Mediator between the disciple and everything else. "Wherever a group, be it large or small, prevents us from standing alone before Christ, wherever such a group raises a claim of immediacy it must be hated for the sake of Christ. For every immediacy, whether we realize it or not, means hatred of Christ, and this is especially true where such relationships claim the sanction of Christian principles."[28]

The mandate of government has been discussed in detail previously. As with business institutions, the disciple cannot relate to government immediately. Christ mediates the relationship. This does not mean that animosity should arise between the disciple and governmental institutions. Government is fulfilling its mandate for our preservation and our good. The governing authorities have the power of the sword at their disposal in order to enforce the laws and regulations thought to be proper. Christians conquer through weakness, through service. These are two different modes of operation. Certainly, Christians in government

---

[27] Dietrich Bonhoeffer, *The Cost of Discipleship* (New York: Simon & Schuster, 1995), 95.
[28] Bonhoeffer, *Discipleship*, 97.

have their own discipleship path which is filled with its own difficulties, in this case, bearing witness to Christ while operating with the power of the sword. Indeed, the world itself operates through the exercise of power in various forms. Government is given the power of the sword which is appropriate to it for the exercise of its own mandate. Apart from this mandated power, there exist all kinds of power games both institutional and personal with which we are familiar. So there is a discernment to be made in action that is proper to the disciple of Christ in terms of proper and improper exercise of power. It is common to hear certain fiery polemics against government in some Christian circles. Perhaps it is a result of resentment against unjust action that has been done. Bonhoeffer has a comment for us at this point.

> How then is it so easy for the Christians to find themselves in opposition to the powers? Because they are so easily tempted to resent their blunders and injustices. But if we harbor such resentments we are in mortal danger of neglecting the will of the God we are called to serve. If only Christians will concentrate on perceiving what is good and on doing it as God commands, they can live "without fear of the authorities."[29]

The disciple of Christ continues to live and proclaim the dominion of Christ over all of life and over all the world. Institutions fulfill the will of God through the mandates by performing the tasks that are proper to those mandates. "The purpose and aim of the dominion of Christ is not to make the worldly order godly or to subordinate it to the

---

[29] Ibid., 97.

church but to set it free for true worldliness."[30] God has called into being institutions under the four mandates. The operations of these institutions are on behalf of the preservation of humankind—the preservation of the world which is created and loved by God. True worldliness makes the disciple's life possible.

To make business into "Christian" business or to make government into "Christian" government is ideology and fanaticism. To accomplish this would require a movement of strength and force thereby robbing the disciple of the privilege of illustrating the weakness of Christ and the weakness of the word. It is enough that secular institutions act with justice within their proper sphere of activity. "We are concerned with secular institutions themselves in accordance with the will of God. We are not interested in "Christianizing" secular institutions, but with their obedience to God's mandates."[31] In receiving protection from government, the disciple and the church-community are grateful and will give government the honor that is its due (Romans 13:7). "To the task of government as such, however, belongs the praise and protection of the godly (1 Peter 2:14), independent of the personal faith of the governmental authorities. Indeed, only in the protection of the godly does government fulfill its true task of serving Christ."[32]

Labor, government and church develop their own institutional forms. Large organizations seem to be typical of

---

[30] Bonhoeffer, *Ethics* 324.
[31] Ibid., 321.
[32] Bonhoeffer, *Conspiracy*, 515.

the age in which we live. The quest to "Christianize" government or business is misplaced. Some non-Christian representatives of government and business do their jobs quite well and for this the church-community should rejoice. It is really an open question whether Christians are equipped to operate in business as well as non-Christians. "For the sons of this world are more shrewd in dealing with their own generation than the sons of light."[33] The Church can rejoice that the institutions within these divine mandates are functioning and that the Church is given space to worship.

---

[33] Luke 16:8.

CHAPTER 6

COMMERCE
AND THE GLORY OF GOD

THE MANDATE OF LABOR has been discussed at length in previous chapters. In this chapter we continue to think about the outworking of this mandate in human society. Although labor, as we know it, lies within the Fall and subsequent cursing of the ground by God, there exist positive consequences of our work. As Bonhoeffer states in *Ethics*, "From the labour which man performs here in fulfillment of the divinely imposed task there arises that likeness of the celestial world by which the man who recognizes Jesus Christ is reminded of the lost Paradise. The first creation of Cain was the city, the earthly counterpart of the eternal city of God."[1] The growth of the city is an

---

[1] Dietrich Bonhoeffer, *Ethics* (New York: Touchstone, 1995), 206.

analogue of the eternal city of God, and St. Augustine states that there is some reciprocal relationship between the two.[2]

Within the city the arts flourish. "There follows the invention of fiddles and flutes, which afford to us on earth a foretaste of the music of heaven."[3] Other heavy industry follows such as mining and extraction. "Next there is the extraction and processing of the metallic treasures from the mines of the earth, partly for the decoration of earthly houses, just as the heavenly city is resplendent with gold and precious stones, and partly for the manufacture of the swords of avenging justice."[4] The extraction of metals from the earth, particularly gold and precious stones, can be used for decoration and the glorification of God specifically through the construction of the Temple and the vesting of the priesthood in the Old Testament and also through the construction of cathedrals and the adornment of churches in the New. Gold and the products of the earth, frankincense and myrrh, are used throughout the biblical story to inform us of the character of the Redeemer. These items are not given to us ready-made, but must be worked up through human labor.

These three products are mentioned many times in the biblical narrative. They are found not only in the story of the Magi, but also in the Song of Solomon and in the instructions for the Temple service in Torah. In biblical

---

[2] [...I will endeavor to treat of the origin, and progress, and deserved destinies of the two cities (the earthly and the heavenly, to wit), which, as we said, are in this present world commingled, and as it were entangled together.] Augustine, *The City of God*, Book XI, Chapter 1.

[3] Bonhoeffer, *Ethics*, 206.

[4] Ibid., 206.

symbolism gold represents kingly rule or purity, frankincense—anointing for the priesthood and prayers of the saints, and myrrh represents the death of Christ. The point is that human labor, business and commerce play a role in the production of these and other commodities and continue to cooperate in the glorification of God through the adoration of the Savior. A brief look at these three products will illustrate the relationship between commerce and the adoration of God, particularly with respect to their mention in Scripture and their production methods.

Gold was abundant in ancient times. The use of it by the ancients was copious also. This included even the gilding of the battlements of cities as stated by Herodotus. The chief sources of gold mentioned in the Old Testament are Arabia, Sheba and Ophir. [5] The Queen of Sheba brought nine thousand pounds of gold along with spices and precious stones as a present for King Solomon. Some commentators think that the Song of Solomon was written in honor of the Queen of Sheba, and we see the theme of gold and spices— frankincense and myrrh—appearing throughout the song. The first mention of gold in the Song is found in Chapter 1. "We will make for you ornaments of gold, studded with silver." [6] Gregory of Elvira, an ancient Spanish Father (c. 392) comments, "We will make you a likeness of gold with chasings of silver—when it says 'gold' is referring to the

---

[5] *Smith's Dictionary of the Bible*, Vol. II, edited by H.B. Hackett (Boston: Houghton, Mifflin and Company, 1889), 936.
[6] Song of Solomon 1:11.

bright splendor of the Holy Spirit. Thus the Magi presented gold to the Lord in order to declare his kingly majesty."[7]

There is an ancient technology of mining gold deposits. Gold was recovered through washing gold-bearing sand in pans or sluices, or by burning fleece that had been saturated with gold-bearing dust in a very high temperature fire. The technology of gold production continues to develop today.

> Extractive metallurgical technologies today can be divided into mineral processing, hydrometallurgy and pyrometallurgy. Mineral processing involves using physical processes to manipulate ore particle size and concentrate valuable minerals through processes of separation. Hydrometallurgy uses liquid solutions to extract metals from ores, such as through leaching, precipitation of insoluble compounds and pressure reduction. Pyrometallurgy treats ores at high temperatures to convert ore minerals to raw metals or intermediate compounds. This involves processes such as roasting, smelting and converting.[8]

There is a current developing technology designed to process Carlin Type gold which "… is a special gold ore, in which gold particles of 0.1 to 0.01 mm in size are disseminated in rock minerals, such as pyrite, illite, and montmorillite. The microsized gold cannot be observed, even with the use of a common microscope, hence the name "invisible gold" or "microsized disseminating gold".[9] Gold

[7] Robert Wilkin, *The Church's Bible: The Song of Songs* (Grand Rapids, MI: William B. Eerdmans Company, 2003), 69.

[8] Available from: http://www.kingsgate.com.au/links/mining-technology-information.htm; Internet.

[9] Available from: http://www.chinatech.com/gold.htm; Internet

production and technology is becoming more sophisticated and complex. Even in the days of the Magi, gold had to be mined, processed, worked into jewelry, and transported. This is a long round-about commercial venture. Through the symbolic nature of this metal, commerce is involved with the glory of God.

Today, gold is used as an aid to worship particularly in Orthodox churches with their gold domes outside and gold adornment inside. This worship space is designed as a representation of the Jerusalem above—Heaven. The Church building becomes a promise of Christ's coming kingdom. Rich and poor alike can rejoice in this space as a reminder of the future fulfillment of all the promises in Scripture.

Likewise frankincense and myrrh have been produced and sold since ancient times. Frankincense is obtained from a white resin from the incised bark of the *Boswellia* tree. It is native to India and Arabia.[10] It seems not to be native to Palestine and in ancient times it was transported from the kingdom of Sheba in southern Arabia from whence the famous Queen of the South traveled to meet Solomon. Frankincense was a key ingredient in making the holy anointing oil for consecrating Aaron and his sons (Exodus 30:34). It was also an integral part of the sacrificial system, and in the Song it is a symbol of luxury or sensuality.[11] Thus, symbolically, frankincense as the gift of the Magi

---

[10] *Fauna and Flora of the Bible*, 2nd edition (New York: United Bible Societies, 1980), 122.

[11] R. Laird Harris, Gleason Archer, and Bruce Waltke, *Theological Wordbook of the Old Testament*, Vol. I (Chicago: Moody Press, 1980), 468.

showed the priesthood of Christ and the ascending prayers of believers, as well as His sensuality or true humanity. Frankincense is still used as a basic incense ingredient in the Orthodox, Catholic, and Anglican churches.

> Frankincense is one of the world's oldest and most famous items of commerce. For over a thousand years, the resin has been carried by camel caravan from the remote harvesting regions in the desert to the far corners of Asia. Navigating by stars, the ancient traders made their way across the sands of the Sahara, following a network of secret cisterns built to collect the precious scanty rain. Every year large shipments of the treasured resin tears found their way into the cities of northern Africa, to be sold in markets from Rome to Beijing. [12]

Commerce in frankincense today begins with harvesting in Somalia, Ethiopia, Yemen, India, or Oman. Sometimes the raw resin is shipped to monasteries to be further processed into cubes that are used for burning in censers. Frankincense continues to fulfill this liturgical function.

Myrrh is native to Arabia, Ethiopia, and the coast of East Africa. It is a resin that exudes from the bark of a bush or tree from the *burseraceae* family which grows in Arabia, but is not native to Palestine. Therefore, this biblical ingredient had to make its way there by caravan. The finest myrrh exudes from the bark without incision having been made previously. This is probably the "liquid myrrh" of the Song. [13] The Apostle John informs us that myrrh was one of the ingredients to be used in embalming the body of Jesus.

---

[12] Available from: http://www.floracopeia.com/content/articles/frankincense; Internet.

[13] *Fauna*, 147.

By ancient consensus of many Church Fathers including Ambrose, Gregory the Great and Gregory of Nyssa, the symbolism of myrrh is associated with death.[14] This could be the death of Christ or the death of the believer with Christ.

Myrrh continues to play an important liturgical role in the Church. The holy oil traditionally used by the Eastern Orthodox Church for performing the sacraments of chrismation and unction is traditionally scented with myrrh, and receiving either of these sacraments is commonly referred to as "receiving the Myrrh."[15] Myrrh is regularly exported by myrrh-producing nations and imported by others. Ethiopia exports more than 70 million tons annually. China has been a major purchaser of myrrh to be used in traditional medicine.

Gold, frankincense and myrrh serve a teaching role throughout Scripture. They formed part of the trading patterns of the ancient world. They continue to be produced and traded in modern commerce. The final word of God speaks of these three products as part of the Babylonian system. In Revelation 17 we see mystery Babylon, a type of religious system that makes war on Christ. In Chapter 18 we see the fall of commercial Babylon. The merchants of the earth were, of course, enriched by the trade and commerce made possible by this antichrist system. There follows a list of all the cargoes that are no longer demanded. These cargoes include gold, frankincense, myrrh and slaves, that is

---

[14] *Ancient Christian Commentary on Scripture*, Vol. IX (Downers Grove, IL: InterVarsity Press, 2005), 345-346.
[15] Available from: http://www.myrrh-oil.org/myrrh.html; Internet.

human souls.[16] God's people are encouraged to "come out of her."[17]

It is here that we need the balance and wisdom of Christ to help us in our life in business. The commercial system traffics in human lives—human souls. These are precious to God, but people are fired and hired every day. This is a type of commerce in human beings. Voluntary bargains are struck, generally speaking, in hiring. This ameliorates the situation. However, in labor markets all over the world a price tag is established for human labor. The commercial system has developed in this way, and it provides most of us with an opportunity to earn our daily bread. Therefore, we give thanks—not to the Babylonian system, but to God who cares for us even in the midst of Babylon.

The products of gold, frankincense and myrrh are produced and traded by commercial Babylon. God has used these materials symbolically throughout history for His glory. So in its trade, Babylon is cooperating in displaying the glory of God. We "come out of her" and remain in her simultaneously. An unquestioning loyalty or love affair with the commercial system is to be avoided. So Eberhard Bethge writes to Dietrich in a letter in 1944 from Italy in the Tiber valley. "And the way the soldiers go through the world, among these people and in this landscape. All they want is for the German police to be here, so that they could see order and work...Some people's delight in commerce is sickening. You can find it in a person right next to

---

[16] Revelation 18:11-13.
[17] Revelation 18:4.

sympathetic qualities: a man with whom you can talk, laugh and steal horses..."[18]

Dietrich also writes in the eschatological vein in describing the end of the world system.

"The old world cannot take pleasure in the Church because the Church speaks of its end as though it had already happened—as though the world had already been judged. The old world does not like being regarded as dead."[19]

In London Bonhoeffer preached to his congregation in 1934 using passages from the prophet Jeremiah. The false prophets are crying "Peace, peace," but there really is no peace in the face of the coming Babylonian invasion. Jeremiah exposes their greed for unjust gain, their luxurious living while deafening themselves to the word of God. The commercial system continued to cooperate by providing objects used in worship, but what use was that? "What use to me is frankincense that comes from Sheba, or sweet cane from a distant land?"[20]

Jeremiah would have been happy to be part of the peace and well-being movement, Bonhoeffer argues, but he could not be part of it. He would have been happy to be loved by his hearers by soothing their emotional unease. "How happy he would have been to have kept quiet and agreed that they were right to say so. But he simply couldn't; he was compelled and under pressure, as if someone were breathing

---

[18] Dietrich Bonhoeffer, *Letters and Papers from Prison* (New York: Touchstone, 1997), 225.

[19] Dietrich Bonhoeffer, *Creation and Fall, Temptation* (New York: Collier Books, 1959), 11.

[20] Jeremiah 6:20.

down his neck and driving him on from one prophecy of truth to the next and from agony to agony." [21] God establishes his prophet to tell the truth about many things, including the life of commerce.

While not operating under divine inspiration, modern whistle-blowers face some of the same pressures as the prophet Jeremiah. After examining marketing documents for a little-known financial firm, Harry Markopolos concluded the reported returns were too good to be true. No firm could turn in that kind of amazing performance year after year. The firm in question was run by Bernard Madoff, the initiator of perhaps the largest Ponzi scheme ever. Markopolos warned the Securities and Exchange Commission for nine years about Madoff's questionable dealings. He said that at times he feared for his life. The nine years of warnings failed to stave off disaster, and investors lost billions of dollars in the ensuing collapse of Madoff's hedge fund. Markopolos is now viewed as a hero, but too late. [22] Whistleblowers should have a place of honor. At the risk at least of their employment, they disclose the truth to anyone who will listen. They reveal illegal or dangerous behavior on the part of various businesses. It seems that there is no end to this struggle to do right with a good will in business. This struggle reveals a problem in the human heart. It is as if we operate under a divine judgment.

In a sermon to his congregation in Barcelona, Bonhoeffer explained. "Culture and religion both stand under divine

[21] Dietrich Bonhoeffer, *London: 1933-1935*, DBWE Vol. 13 (Minneapolis, MN: Fortress Press, 2007), 351.
[22] *USA Today*, February 13, 2009, Money Section.

judgment." [23] God has made a path to human beings through Incarnation, Atonement and Resurrection. Other attempts to bring an offering to God through religion or business must be just that—attempts.

> One question forces itself upon us now. Is it all over for our religion and our morality, if none of that can lead us to God and if God's paths are indeed different from our paths: Certainly not, for we are called to serve the God who gives us grace. Our religious and moral life, which is now placed under God's judgment and which has become transparent as human, all too human, is our attempt to present an offering to God. But it remains merely an attempt and nothing more, and whoever would make more of it is choosing the path toward God anew, the Tower of Babel....And yet as long as there is grace, they remain necessary as a weak attempt, as a representation, as an offering to which God can say yes or no as he pleases. [24]

God has established the mandate of labor. He has given us tasks to do in order to stay occupied in them. He is pleased to use from time to time the products of our hands in worship and in teaching. In this sense, the world system, Babylon, gives glory to God. The world of commerce with all of its sharp practice, its deceit, its heartache also serves God. Offenses against God occur every day in business as in all other areas of life. However, "Not every offence against the divine task must in itself on principle deprive of their divine mandate the concrete forms of labour, marriage,

---

[23] Dietrich Bonhoeffer, *Barcelona, Berlin, New York: 1928-1931*, DBWE Vol. 10 (Minneapolis, MN: Fortress Press, 2008), 483.

[24] Bonhoeffer, *Barcelona*, 483.

government and church."[25] Wrong actions do not invalidate any of the mandates in which we operate.

What is needed here is an understanding of the divine purposes involved in the tasks of labor. There is more involved in my vocation than work and creativity. Work in the world is an important element in the formation of Christ in us. The goal of the mandates is Christ Himself. Therefore, we can develop a new way of seeing the purpose of our work. "This genuine responsibility consists in the adaptation of the concrete form of the divine mandates to their origin, their continuance and their goal in Jesus Christ."[26] Commerce not only glorifies God with the products it produces, it provides a concrete situation in which Christ's character may be formed in us.

[25] Bonhoeffer, *Ethics*, 205.
[26] Ibid., 206.

CHAPTER 7

BUSINESS AS THE VOID

IN THE WINTER semester of 1932-1933 Dietrich Bonhoeffer delivered a series of lectures to his students at the University of Berlin. These lectures have been published from student notes under the title *Creation and Fall*. In them we encounter some heavy discussion on creation and the void. Perhaps some explanation here will provide an appropriate backdrop for the title of this chapter.

> In the beginning God created the heavens and the earth. That means that the Creator, in freedom, creates the creature. Their *connexion* is not conditioned by anything except freedom, which means that it is unconditioned....Creator and creature cannot be said to have relation of cause and effect, for between Creator and creature there is neither a law of motive nor a law of effect nor anything else. Between Creator and creature there is simply nothing: the void. For freedom happens in and through the void. There is no necessity that can be shown in God which can or must ensue in creation. There is

nothing that causes him to create. Creation comes out of this void.[1]

Bonhoeffer explains that our thought about the void begins to be confused when we are unable to think of a beginning. If we cannot do that, then the void itself, or nothingness becomes the source of existence; it becomes creative. This may be a reason that nihilism gains a foothold among us. If nothingness is our source, then we must be nothing also. This is a last attempt at explanation for the persons who cannot conceive of or affirm a beginning. This void does not explain creation. It does not provide a ground for creation, but in the beginning God creates the universe and simultaneously creates and overcomes the void. The void is nothing, and God created it and overcame it. "The void contains no anxiety for the first creation. On the contrary, it is itself the eternal song praising the Creator who created the world out of nothing. The world stands in the void. This means that it stands in the beginning; and that means nothing except that it is rooted in the freedom of God. The creature belongs to the Creator."[2]

When theology proclaims that God has created "ex nihilo" (from nothing) the emphasis is on God, not on the nothing. "In the beginning, God created the heavens and the earth."[3] The universe is real because it was created by God. Therefore, in working up the materials of the universe into products we are engaged in real action. Business is not

---

[1] Dietrich Bonhoeffer, *Creation and Fall: Temptation* (New York: Macmillan Publishing Company, 1953), 18.

[2] Bonhoeffer, *Creation and Fall*, 19.

[3] Genesis 1:1.

simply an existential refuge with no blessing and no meaning. It is not a void in imitation of the primal void. The world of work has certain solid benefits which have been enumerated in previous chapters. Even the primal void, like all things, awaits God's action and serves God's glory. Our world, which is not the void, proclaims God's glory. Perhaps the rabbinical tradition of creation is better here which sees the letters of the Hebrew alphabet as being the primal building blocks of the universe. This gives more emphasis to the word of God as being creative—not the void.

There is a kind of intellectual malaise afoot which manifests itself in nihilism or a kind of existentialism in which we authenticate ourselves through the decisions we make and the actions we take. The decisions and the actions in this mode of thought are meaningless in themselves, but provide a so-called authentic experience for the individual. This (perhaps frenetic) action is undertaken to avoid a blacker form of nihilism—a belief that nothing can be known and no meaning can be discerned in life as we know it. This view could lead to the plunge into business as existentialist action or simply as another form of nihilism. This would lead to business as the void—either to be jumped into with fanaticism or endured with resignation. But this is not labor as mandated by God.

It is possible for a Christian to move into this type of existentialist thinking. An all-embracing love of business can lead us into the void. By this I mean that the death of our Christ-life is in view when this other love consumes us. An all-embracing life of business can be lived as an existentialist answer to meaning. We can simply choose this path as the only path of meaning. In his book *The Cost of Discipleship*, Dietrich Bonhoeffer says this, "Our hearts have room only for one all-embracing devotion, and we can only cleave to one Lord. Every competitor to that devotion must be hated. As Jesus says, there is no alternative—either we love God or we hate him."[4] However, the human heart hankers after a treasure and glory, and God graciously accommodates us. "It is to be observed that Jesus does not deprive the human heart of its instinctive needs—treasure, glory and praise. But he gives it higher objects—the glory of God (John 5:44), the glorying in the cross (Gal. 6:14), and the treasure in heaven."[5]

Bonhoeffer encouraged his Finkenwalde students who had been conscripted into military service concerning their Christ-life. Surely the soldier's life, like the businessperson's life, can be so filled with activity that the Christ-life becomes far away. We may feel as if we are moving into the void, but there is a way that God comes to us and preserves us.

> Whereas those of us in the ministry are reminded of being a Christian constantly throughout the day, for you hours and whole days may go by without any moment for such recollections, just as is the case for most working people. If then, some morning or evening or at some unexpected hour, the moment for such recollection comes—and it will come—then it is often so overwhelming that we can hardly bear it;....God knows your present life and finds a way to

---

[4] Dietrich Bonhoeffer, *The Cost of Discipleship* (New York: Touchstone, 1995), 176.
[5] Bonhoeffer, *Discipleship*, 176.

you even in the most strained and overburdened days, when you can no longer find the way to God.[6]

An embracing of the void makes the void into god. Business could become a god. Without a belief in the beginning, business could become an existential pursuit with certain possible payoffs such as pleasure, health, and security.

> "…[L]ife fluctuates between the most bestial enjoyment of the moment and an adventurous game of chance. An abrupt end is put to any kind of inner self-development and to any gradual attainment of personal or vocational maturity. There is no personal destiny, and consequently there is no personal dignity."[7]

Two things can prevent this grim scenario from coming to pass. One is the awakening of faith.

Dietrich had hope for a recovery of faith even in a world given to nihilism. In a letter to the Leibolz family in England he writes about his hope that his niece Marianne will make her way to Christ through her involvement in the Methodist Church. "There are so many experiences and disappointments which make a way for nihilism and resignation for sensitive people. So it is good to learn early enough that suffering and God is not a contradiction but rather a necessary unity; for me the idea that God himself is suffering has always been one of the most convincing teachings of Christianity. I think God is nearer to suffering than to happiness and to find God in this way gives peace

---

[6] Dietrich Bonhoeffer, *Conspiracy and Imprisonment: 1940 – 1945*, DBWE Vol. 16 (Minneapolis, MN: Fortress Press, 2006), 47.
[7] Dietrich Bonhoeffer, *Ethics* (New York: Touchstone, 1995), 107.

and rest and a strong and courageous heart."[8] Not only do people suffer in their rejection of the Creator, but God is suffering along with them. Wrong action in the business world is not evidence against the love of Christ or for nihilism. The disciple in business can deal with goods and preserve singlenesss of heart for Christ who was a person like us who had bodily needs. "Jesus does not forbid the possession of property in itself. He was a man, he ate and drank like his disciples, and thereby sanctified the good things of life. These necessities, which are consumed in use and which meet the legitimate requirements of the body, are to be used by the disciple with thankfulness."[9]

The other preventative of the plunge into the void is the restraining power of government, or at least government can prevent some of the worst effects of embracing the void. Recent experience shows that government must regulate some markets simply to restrain evil, in this case the bizarre financial dealings of many. For example, the development of a series of very complicated financial derivative packages may be partly responsible for the worldwide recession of 2008-2009. These financial instruments were difficult to evaluate containing as they did a variety of mortgages and other financial paper. When the housing market slowed and went sour in the US, these billions of dollars of investments became impossible to evaluate thus the resulting slowdown in banking activity and credit markets. Government must now step in to restrain the madness of this esoteric development, as well as multi-billion dollar Ponzi schemes

---

[8] Bonhoeffer, *Conspiracy*, 284.
[9] Bonhoeffer, *Discipleship*, 174.

in order to shore up confidence in the banking system and financial markets in general. Government, in this case, prevents a fall into financial oblivion.

"For the mystery of lawlessness is already at work. Only he who now restrains it will do so until he is out of the way." [10] The restraint of evil by government is the interpretation placed upon this passage by centuries of Church teaching and also by Bonhoeffer. Government provides a restraining force against evil until the apocalyptic time when government itself becomes too evil to function.

A good example of business as the void is given in the famous play by Arthur Miller, *The Death of a Salesman.* Willy Loman, the salesman, is asking his friend Charley for a loan to pay his insurance premium. Willy is concerned if he has raised his boys correctly and asks Charley if he ever took any interest in his own son, to which Charley replies, "My salvation is that I never took any interest in anything. There's some money—fifty dollars. I got an accountant inside." [11] In this case, salvation is not taking an interest in anything. This is life in the void. Since there is nothing, there is nothing in which to take an interest, and the sooner that Willy realizes this, the better off he will be—this is Charley's opinion.

---

[10] 2 Thessalonians 2:7.
[11] Arthur Miller, *Death of a Salesman*, edited by Gerald Weales (New York: The Viking Press, 1968), 96.

Business as a Penultimate Pursuit

IN HIS BOOK *Ethics*, Bonhoeffer presents life and thought as moving between two limits, the ultimate word of God and the penultimate word of God. The ultimate word of God is the word of the last things—an eschatological word. It is also the word of justification, of grace and faith alone. This ultimate word of God makes our daily round of activities appear to be small, useless, and perhaps blasphemous. However, there is a penultimate word of God in which various duties are enjoined upon us. The penultimate word of God refers to the things before the last things. We have vocations to fulfill before the end comes, and these vocations and works, since enjoined by Christ, have value before God. Both of these limits are true. An emphasis on the ultimate word of God is the radical solution; all actions are placed within the framework of final judgment. An emphasis on the penultimate word of God is the compromise solution in which daily activities are emphasized as part of the mandate of labor and of human life in general. The solution of life within these limits is found in the life of Christ, because, "...in Jesus Christ there is neither radicalism nor compromise, but there is the reality of God and men."[12]

Business is one of those penultimate things. There are tasks to perform that are enjoined upon us as followers of Christ. There are others for whom I am providing and caring. Business provides the means for my doing so. Christ assumes that parents know how to give good things to their children. So we work, produce and give. Jesus uses examples

---

[12] Bonhoeffer, *Ethics*, 128.

from business to teach various parables such as the merchant seeking pearls, the buyer of a field containing great treasure and the employer discussing wage rates with his workers. In other words, business life is expected, normal life in the Scriptures. The problem in discussing the ultimate and the penultimate word of God is that the upbuilding of one side involves a sort of radical break with the other side. The resolution can be seen only in Christ. Business is a penultimate pursuit. We find ourselves there. However, the ultimate word must be lived in the business world also. The word of grace, faith and justification sustains me in the midst of a perplexing moral dilemma. God's grace gives me hope as I work at an apparently meaningless task. God's love sustains me in the midst of a hostile situation, and the eschatological word may also give me joy amidst the burdens of the day. Georg Huntemann comments on Bonhoeffer's work here, "Thus all reality, even that which is hostile to God and in which God appears powerless, is brought under the triumph of Christ that will be revealed at the end of time. Nothing is in vain, nothing is lost, no eternal abyss of nothingness threatens—at the second coming every pain, every death, every tear will make sense."[13]

It is in the business world that an opportunity is opened for the new life of Christ to break in on a situation which has already been judged and condemned by the death of Christ. "In Christ, the reality of God meets the reality of the world and allows us to share in this real encounter."[14] God

---

[13] Georg Huntemann, *Dietrich Bonhoeffer: An Evangelical Reassessment*, trans. by Todd Huizinga (Grand Rapids, MI: Baker Books, 1996), 160.
[14] Bonhoeffer, *Ethics*, 132.

says "yes" to our decision-making struggles because of the incarnation, and because God says "yes", final judgment must be left to Him. This, therefore, is not ideological action which is always self-justified. Ideological action follows its own programme, its own principle, and by realizing its programme it is therefore justified. Discipleship is not programmatic, but responsible action which lays no claim to its ultimate righteousness. Thus, Eberhard Bethge comments on Dietrich's teaching at the Finkenwalde seminary.

> The call of Jesus cannot be turned into a program or an ideology; indeed, that would mean a failure of discipleship, for discipleship means breaking away from casuistic and legalistic programs. To be called to go, and to follow—this is a true Christology. To be called and not to follow, but instead to work out a program for use in this or that situation—this is a false Christology. It leaves Christ out in the cold as an occasional aid toward salvation.[15]

In the context of business, Bethge and Bonhoeffer are saying that the businessperson simply brings the reality of Christ into the workplace. There is not a previously worked out plan of how the reality of Christ will be lived, and there is no necessary pietistic phrase that is used to inform people that Christ is here. Christ is not brought in as an add-on, but Christ lives his life through the businessperson.

Even in prison Dietrich tried to live the reality of a follower of Christ. In prison when one has the prospect of death very close at hand, it would seem that ultimate

---

[15] Eberhard Bethge, *Dietrich Bonhoeffer: A Biography* (Minneapolis, MN: Fortress Press, 2000), 455.

considerations would continually be at the forefront of thinking. That is probably true, but Dietrich, at the same time maintained hope and a lively interest in the penultimate things—the things before the last thing. His upcoming wedding with Maria occupied much of his thought and gave him great joy. "However fanciful I currently find my secret hope that some time—when?—we shall all celebrate my and Maria's wedding day together, it's a great and wonderful thought."[16]

Eberhard Bethge said that Dietrich wrote and preached some of the best wedding sermons of the day. This was precisely because of his love of life and his hope in Christ and in the future. In an earlier letter to his friend, Gustav Seydel, one of the Finkenwalde seminarians, Dietrich sent this wedding greeting in 1942.

> As earthly human beings, we have to take account of an earthly future. For the sake of this future we must accept tasks, responsibilities, and joys and sorrows. We need not despise happiness simply because there is so much unhappiness. We should not arrogantly push away the kind hand of God because God's hand is otherwise so hard. I think it is more important to remind one another of this in these days than of many other things, and I received your wedding announcement gratefully as a fine testimony to this very thing.[17]

Since we live in the era before the last things, Bonhoeffer would encourage us to enjoy the happiness that God gives us today. There will be unhappiness enough another day. To

[16] Ruth-Alice von Bismarck and Ulrich Kabitz, *Love Letters from Cell 92* (Nashville, TN: Abingdon Press, 1995), 22.
[17] Bonhoeffer, *Conspiracy*, 328.

this the words of Scripture agree. "In the day of prosperity be joyful, and in the day of adversity consider: God has made the one as well as the other,..."[18]

The Success Syndrome

THE SUCCESS SYNDROME is everywhere—in marriage, labor, government and church. It makes sense. I am not exactly striving for failure. In business there are different levels of success. At the most basic level a certain minimum level of profits must be earned in order for the business to maintain itself as a going concern. This provides a living for owners and workers alike. A business might earn a higher level of profits which can promote expansion, higher incomes and perhaps more employees. No doubt, there is a certain amount of prestige attached to these higher profit rates. There is a human tendency to strive for prestige and praise. Is the success syndrome, therefore, a law of life?

Without the goals of achievement and success, or the success syndrome, there is a danger that life will become incomprehensible. This law is not administered by governmental units nor by the Church, yet it seems to have a very tight grip upon the imagination. The problem with this law is that there seems to be something wrong with it even as it is slavishly obeyed. To fail in the achievement of success places one outside of normal society. Therefore,

---

[18] Ecclesiastes 7:14.

there is a conflict within the human being as we strive to obey this law while knowing that it is not totally right.

Do failures have the right to live? No, was the attitude of the Nationalist Socialist government of Bonhoeffer's day, as seen by their extermination camps reserved for the socially unfit according to Nazi standards. Certainly failures do have the right to live, but perhaps there needs to be a clearer articulation of the meaning of failure and the meaning of success and a clearer statement of the church's teaching on this matter.

As a Christmas gift to General Oster and Hans von Dohnanyi, his colleagues in the *Abwehr*, Bonhoeffer wrote a piece entitled "After Ten Years: A Reckoning made at New Year 1943" in which he discusses the matter of success for his friends. Success is not ethically neutral, or perhaps it could be as long as good is successful. When evil is successful our cooperation in a project or our refusal becomes more important. In this case success is not ethically neutral, but a case for reflection and decision-making. Perhaps we tend to uncritically approve success in all its forms because of actions of various members of the Church.

Some think that various kinds of spectacular works or spectacular projects that could be organized and performed by the Church would be the way to influence large numbers of people for the gospel. Maybe there is something to this. However, Bonhoeffer counters with this, "...the church that wants to become the church of God's visible glory, here and now, has denied its Lord on the cross."[19] Bonhoeffer likes to

---

[19] Dietrich Bonhoeffer, *London, 1933-1935*, DBWE Vol. 13 (Minneapolis: Fortress Press, 2007), 396.

emphasize the Church's ministry through the weakness of the word. Success can become an ideology. The Church may have a part in this through certain perspectives on carrying the gospel into the world.

> "...[Z]eal which refuses to take note of resistance springs from a confusion of the gospel with a victorious ideology. An ideology requires fanatics who neither know nor notice opposition, and it is certainly a potent force. But the word of God in its weakness takes the risk of meeting the scorn of men and being rejected."[20]

In our zeal to present the gospel, we need to be careful that we present the Savior as a real man, not simply an idea-man—an ideology. "To try and force the Word on the world by hook or by crook is to make the living Word of God into a mere idea...."[21]

Bonhoeffer presents the radical and compromise solutions with respect to success. The radical solution is simply to criticize, and the compromise solution is to be an opportunist. Obviously, a sounder position is needed. With respect to business the question for the disciple is not how to extricate himself heroically from the problem, but how is the coming generation to live?[22] How are my children going to live? There are two considerations here. One is physical survival through labor and business. The other is the character that my children will develop. How will their character be formed through my action? Our decision here

---

[20] Bonhoeffer, *Discipleship*, 186.
[21] Ibid., 187.
[22] Dietrich Bonhoeffer, *Letters and Papers from Prison* (New York: Simon & Schuster, 1997), 7.

will be made evident through our action. It will be made in concrete responsibility. "In short, it is much easier to see a thing through from the point of view of abstract principle than from that of concrete responsibility."[23]

Most people apprehend the laws of good moral behavior whether from the Ten Commandments or not. Most people apprehend that some kind of moral universe is in place. This means that if good moral principles are broken an adverse result is the likely eventuality. This knowledge may put a brake upon our uncritical allegiance to the success syndrome. Human reason may lead us to this point. However, this is not the main point of the Ten Commandments which speak from beyond human reason. Reason might indicate that the Ten Commandments are given to us simply as part of the tool kit of success. "Not so," is Bonhoeffer's response.

> God, on the other hand, does not speak of life and its successes and failures; rather, God speaks of God's own self. God's first word in the Ten Commandments is 'I.' human beings are confronted with this 'I,' not with some sort of general law—not with 'one should do this or that,' but with the living God. In every word of the Ten Commandments, God speaks fundamentally of God's self, and this is their main point. That is why they are God's revelation. It is not a law but God we are obeying in the Ten Commandments, and our failure when we break them comes not from disobeying a law but from disobeying God. Transgressors face not merely disorder and failure but the wrath of God. It is not merely unwise to disregard God's command; it is sin, and the wages of sin are death. This is the reason the

---

[23] Bonhoeffer, *Letters and Papers*, 7.

New Testament calls the Ten Commandments 'living words' (Acts 7:38).[24]

The Idolization of Success

THE SUCCESS of my boss is my concern. I share in rejoicing over a good profit picture for the firm which is an analogue for a good return on spiritual gifts, as in the parable of the talents. As already mentioned, profits must attain at least a certain minimum. Higher profit rates allow certain good and legitimate results for the business. We are, obviously, striving for the success of our business, but we must guard against a pitfall here. The snare is the idolization of success.

Some businesspersons speaking to university student groups motivate students toward the Christ life; others motivate toward success only. It is the latter which bring a danger to campus. Indeed vast parts of the church have woven the message of success into the fabric of their proclamation so that the figure of the Crucified is hardly recognizable. In this gospel of success, "Success is simply identified with good. This attitude is genuine and pardonable only in a state of intoxication."[25]

The cult of success can blind us to the straightforward path of doing the right thing. The clear difference between fair play and foul play becomes not so clear when analyzed in light of overwhelming success. We do well in the business school to look past the lionization of successful

---

[24] Bonhoeffer, *Conspiracy*, 634.
[25] Bonhoeffer, *Ethics*, 78.

businesspersons, and not assume that whatever they have done in their business demonstrates the reality of God. Another variation on this theme is the proposition that only good is successful. This would entail another approach by the Christian business ethicist that the practice of biblical teaching, for example in the Book of Proverbs, will bring success in business. This may be somewhat true or largely true, but certainly there are cases where the winsome Christian through biblical practice did not achieve business success although all the right things were being done. "Again I saw that under the sun the race is not to the swift, nor the battle to the strong, nor bread to the wise, nor riches to the intelligent, nor favor to those with knowledge, but time and chance happen to them all." [26] Success does not automatically bring moral approbation or Christlikeness. To treat it so, is to make an idol out of success.

Bonhoeffer is obviously against this. Success is not the standard but the figure of the Crucified. On the other hand failure is not the standard either. Christ being revealed in me as I work for the success of the business is the divine reality breaking through into me and our world. Nor should there be a desire to be good for its own sake as a vocation. Business is my vocation, and the revelation of Christ in me is the ground of all my ethical reflection. "A desire to be good for its own sake, as an end in itself, so to speak, or as a vocation in life, falls victim to the irony of unreality. The genuine striving for good now becomes the self-assertiveness of the prig. Good is not in itself an independent theme for

---

[26] Ecclesiastes 9:11.

life; if it were so it would be the craziest kind of quixotry. Only if we share in reality can we share in good."[27]

Reality for many of us is our life in business. Success becomes at least—shall we say—a goal. It may be only a short step from this point to the making of success into an idol. Bonhoeffer argues that this is really the modern—the post-modern—temptation toward idolatry. Success is one of several idols at which the heart of humans has worshipped. In the increasingly nihilistic world of the Third Reich, success was one of the few gods left to many people.

> We are now accustomed to saying our gods are money, sensuality, honor, other people, ourselves. It would be more accurate if we were to characterize power, success, the development of strength as our gods....Our very being has gone too far off track still to be capable of having idols and worshiping them. If we still have an idol, it is perhaps nothingness, extinction, meaninglessness. Thus the First Commandment calls us to the one true God, the almighty, just, and merciful one who rescues us from falling prey to nothingness and sustains us in God's own church-community.[28]

So we live truly in the world—the business world—striving, working, setting goals. However, in the midst of all this mundane calculation we are aware that we stand before God continually. This is part of Bonhoeffer's secular interpretation of Christianity. What better place to think about this than in business? The "religious" interpretation looks to the power of God in the world and calls for help

---

[27] Bonhoeffer, *Ethics*, 189.
[28] Bonhoeffer, *Conspiracy*, 638.

when business problems are overwhelming or the plan is failing. This is a sort of "God of the gaps" approach. Philosophically, God is used to fill in or explain gaps in knowledge. In business, God is invoked to solve my problem. Bonhoeffer would raise the question as to how we will relate to God if science explains all the questions. How will we relate to God if business is running smoothly?

The "non-religious" interpretation allows us to immerse ourselves completely in secular pursuits (like business). This is how we participate in the suffering of God. In that very moment we know that God is ministering to us in weakness. That is how God helps us. Christ helps us by virtue of His weakness and suffering. St. Matthew quotes from the prophet Isaiah in his gospel and applies the Old Testament prophecy to Christ, "Surely he has borne our griefs and carried our sorrows; yet we esteemed him stricken, smitten by God, and afflicted. But he was wounded for our transgressions;..."[29] It is therefore only by living completely in the world of business that one learns to have faith. "How can success make us arrogant, or failure lead us astray, when we share in God's sufferings through a life of this kind?"[30]

Failure in Business

UNEMPLOYMENT AND BUSINESS failures are personal and corporate tragedies. The desire and responsibility to work and provide for loved ones is either threatened or taken

---

[29] Isaiah 53:4-5.
[30] Bonhoeffer, *Letters and Papers*, 370.

away. Perhaps these terrible possibilities show us the positive side of striving for success. The life that Bonhoeffer is discussing is in some ways beyond failure and success, but there is a clear recognition that the good things of life are blessings from God and should be enjoyed. "It is striking to many earnest Christians as they pray the Psalms how frequently there occurs a petition for life and good fortune. When looking at the cross of Christ there arises in many the unhealthy thought that life and the visible earthly blessings of God are in themselves certainly a questionable good and in any case not to be desired."[31] This is the morose version of the Christian life where any kind of bodily enjoyment is suspect. Dietrich treats this in the section "The Right to Bodily Life" in *Ethics*. As discussed previously, there is some clear teaching in the book of Ecclesiastes on the joys of life that the Creator has bestowed on many. However, there is a connection between our daily bread, simple joys and labor. Business failure is a tragedy that is rightly sought to be remedied by labor, business and government.

Dietrich wished to be working, helping his family and others as the political-military- economic situation collapsed around everyone in Germany. In a letter to his parents he states, "The stormy happenings in the world in the last few days go right through one, and I wish I could be doing useful service somewhere or other, but at present that 'somewhere' must be in the prison cell, and what I can do

---

[31] Dietrich Bonhoeffer, *Prayerbook of the Bible: An Introduction to the Psalms*, DBWE Vol. 5 (Minneapolis, MN: Fortress Press, 2005), 168.

here makes its contribution in the unseen world, a sphere where the word 'do' is quite unsuitable."[32]

In his little book *Prayerbook of the Bible: An Introduction to the Psalms*, Bonhoeffer points out that there is not a quick and easy surrender to suffering by the Psalmist. Faith is strained when the wicked go free and the righteous suffer. However, in the midst of distress and hopelessness it is God that is continually addressed. The prayers of the Psalms are seeking for the One who has borne our griefs. Only he has experienced all of it, and he can help us.[33]

Eberhard Bethge discusses Bonhoeffer's thought concerning the way that Jesus is present to us in "religionless Christianity."

1. Jesus does not call for any acceptance of preliminary systems of thought and behavior;

2. He is anti-individualist, unprotected, and, in a totally vulnerable fashion, the man for others;

3. He does not pray as if prayer were a partial payment on the installment plan, but with his life;

4. He turns away from the temptation of [God as] *deus ex machina* [God out of the machine or God simply coming on stage to solve our problems];

5. He turns away from the privileged classes and sits together with the outcasts; and

---

[32] Bonhoeffer, *Letters and Papers*, 109.
[33] Bonhoeffer, *Prayerbook*, 169-170.

159

6. He liberates us to find our own responsible answer to life through his own powerlessness, which shames and utterly convinces us.[34]

How is Jesus with us in our time of failure? Bonhoeffer's insights here can help us to think more soberly, wisely, and hopefully in our time of success and failure. In his prison correspondence with Eberhard Bethge, Bonhoeffer mentions what he has received and his formation thereby. "It's through what he himself is, plus what he receives, that a man becomes a complete entity. I wanted to tell you this, because I've now experienced it for myself,..."[35] In his moving Christmas correspondence of 1942 to General Oster and Hans von Dohnanyi, Dietrich mentions his great spiritual growth and formation through his experience of imprisonment and deprivation. He mentions new, truer perspectives that he has gained through this terrible ordeal. These perspectives could have been gained in no other way. A section from this famous correspondence is worth quoting in full. Here we see the extent of Bonhoeffer's character development into the image of Christ brought about through his moral suffering as a member of the conspiracy.

The view from below

THERE REMAINS an experience of incomparable value. We have for once learnt to see the great events of world history

---

[34] Eberhard Bethge, *Dietrich Bonhoeffer: A Biography* (Minneapolis, MN: Fortress Press, 2000), 878.
[35] Bonhoeffer, *Letters and Papers*, 150.

from below, from the perspective of the outcast, the suspects, the maltreated, the powerless, the oppressed, the reviled—in short, from the perspective of those who suffer. The important thing is that neither bitterness nor envy should have come to look with new eyes at matters great and small, sorrow and joy, strength and weakness, that our perception of generosity, humanity, justice and mercy should have become clearer, freer, less corruptible. We have to learn that personal suffering is a more effective key, a more rewarding principle for exploring the world in thought and action than personal good fortune. This perspective from below must not become the partisan possession of those who are eternally dissatisfied; rather, we must do justice to life in all its dimensions from a higher satisfaction, whose foundation is beyond any talk of 'from below' or 'from above'. This is the way in which we may affirm it.[36]

---

[36] Bonhoeffer, *Letters and Papers*, 17.

CHAPTER 8

VOCATION

OUR VOCATION HAS to do with our working life. Vocation comes from the Latin word *vocare*, "to call." From this derivation we also speak occasionally of work as a calling. God is calling us into the world of work, but how? Just as we cannot express an authoritative formula for attaining faith, so we cannot express a rule for finding vocation. Bonhoeffer emphasizes the role that passion can play in giving us a life task. Passion or a strong interest leads us to submerge ourselves in something else. Perhaps this something else could be someone else, as in, a lover. Perhaps it could be building or repairing with the materials of the earth. Perhaps it could be designing or solving scientific problems. Perhaps it could be serving, interacting with people, or working in nature. The idea is to be overcome by this thing or person and submerged therein, thereby overcoming some of our ego-centeredness.

Vocation can also become routine, deadening and soul-destroying. As with all things, work or vocation is a two-edged sword. Bonhoeffer emphasizes the danger of becoming like the machines that we employ (Adam Smith saw the same danger). The bureaucratization of work can also dampen our zeal for vocation.

> The God-willed meaning of every passion, a passion for one's vocation, for another person, is that in it our self submerges and by submerging is created anew, that the soul is cleansed where it is extinguished by something other than itself to which it surrenders itself. Here we find the inexhaustible blessing of our vocational work, and here also the curse weighing upon the machine, which turns those who must work at it day after day into part of the mechanism themselves, a mechanism with which they can never develop a personally passionate relationship.[1]

Vocation is not "...that pseudo-Lutheran view for which the concept of vocation simply provides the justification and sanctification of secular institutions."[2] However, God seeks us and finds us in a place of work or vocation. As a worker who hears the call of Christ to Himself and to discipleship, my work truly becomes a calling. In other words, in this sense, the work or the vocation can come before the calling. Christ makes the job into a calling. There is no necessary religious experience that will definitively place us in a vocation. We make vocational choices based on many factors. When Christ finds us in our vocation, this does not

---

[1] Dietrich Bonhoeffer, *Barcelona, Berlin, New York, 1928-1931*, DBWE Vol. 10 (Minneapolis: Fortress Press, 2008), 533.
[2] Dietrich Bonhoeffer, *Ethics* (New York: Touchstone, 1995), 250.

mean that we have to look for a more "spiritual" life or vocation. To this the words of the Apostle agree, "So, brothers, in whatever condition each was called, there let him remain with God."[3]

The life of Christ in vocation gives me true responsibility. Responsibility avoids two extremes. One extreme view would be that in simply fulfilling my duties exactly and in a limited way that my duty is discharged. But the life of Christ, the call of Christ summons us to a further walk with Christ. The call also lies behind these duties. "The calling, in the New Testament sense, is never a sanctioning of worldly institutions as such; its 'yes' to them always includes at the same time an extremely emphatic 'no,' an extremely sharp protest against the world."[4] This is the familiar "in the world but not of it" teaching of Christ which is the strange position in which we find ourselves in vocation.

The second extreme position is the attempt to find a place that is not the world. The vocational call will not land us in a place that is not the world. Even a cave in the wilderness is located in the world with the attendant problems brought on by the Fall, and surely the monastery is also part of the world. In this sense, there can be a proper monastic vocation for the person who recognizes his or her position in the world and Christ's "yes" and "no" to it. The monastic vocation is in the world, but not of it. Both businessman and monk can make use of the world without withdrawing from it. Either one could retreat more from the

---

[3] 1 Corinthians 7:24.
[4] Bonhoeffer, *Ethics*, 251.

world or go into it more fully depending on Christ's will and plan for their discipleship.

In describing some interrelated themes of the latter part of Bonhoeffer's prison correspondence, Eberhard Bethge mentions the famous phrases "the world come of age, nonreligious interpretation, and the arcane discipline." We have mentioned some of these themes in earlier chapters. However, "the world come of age" has particular relevance for our discussion of vocation. This phrase does not mean that the world has somehow become better. It refers to a development among people and nations to exercise their own autonomy, intellect and will—a desire to exercise self responsibility without the tutelage of, say, the Church, or God. This, says Bonhoeffer, is the movement of the modern world. In short, there is an increasing secularization of life.

There is no despair here, however. "The world come of age" was a necessary part of Bonhoeffer's Christology. Within the secularization of life the crucified and risen Christ is Lord over the world and the vocations in it. This gives us the opportunity and ability to participate in "true worldliness." Therefore, I am free to engage the world by pursuing my vocation with a good will. Bethge states, "Bonhoeffer's theme entails setting out in order to discover the presence of Christ in the world of today: it is not a discovery of the modern world, nor a discovery of Christ from this modern world, but discovering *him* in this world."[5] With this the Book of Proverbs agrees as Wisdom lifts up her voice in the marketplace, in the noisy streets, and

---

[5] Eberhard Bethge, *Dietrich Bonhoeffer: A Biography* (Minneapolis, MN: Fortress Press, 2000), 865-866.

in the city. She invites everyone to listen to her counsel. The wise man invites us to seek for wisdom which includes our life in vocation and life in the city. It is here that we find the knowledge of God (Proverbs 1 and 2).

God places his "yes" on work and vocation already in the garden of Eden, but doubly so in the Incarnation. After all, Christ was a carpenter. The call of Christ through vocation is a call to Christ Himself. Through being called to Christ in my vocation I develop a certain surety and confidence of decision-making in concrete cases knowing that I am commissioned by Christ and working for Christ. However, as this call develops, there comes a point of definite break with the past—a costly affirmation of Christ's lordship over us. Bonhoeffer calls this the first step which creates a new situation and makes it impossible for us to stay in the old situation of discipleship. "Unless a definite step is demanded, the call vanishes into thin air, and if men imagine that they can follow Jesus without taking this step, they are deluding themselves like fanatics."[6]

One of the definite steps came to me around three decades ago. I was working as a professor at a small college at which everything was going well. One day the president of the college approached me and said that he was expecting me to talk with the pastor of my local church about further financial support for the college. Now, this might be alright. This might be the right thing to do. However, in this case it struck me as being wrong. I assured the president that I would do exactly what he had requested and went on my

[6] Dietrich Bonhoeffer, *The Cost of Discipleship* (New York: Simon & Schuster, 1995), 63.

way. So far, so good—I could have let the matter drop there and simply not done what I said I would do, and that would have solved the problem. I have done things like that before and may again.

However, when I returned to my office I felt as if the Holy Spirit were reminding me of the need to live with integrity. I had lied to the president, and I needed to make it right. I realized that what I was about to do was potentially very costly. So, I went to the president's office and told him that I didn't want to deal with him on false pretenses. I had no intention of talking with my pastor about finances. Great bombast followed between the president and myself. Later, my situation grew dark. Worry took over my mind. What Christ had me to do created a new situation of discipleship for me. I was conscious of belonging to Christ more directly and more completely. The step was costly, and I am grateful that I am still in the professoriate. I certainly did not devise this situation or scenario. Evidently, Christ devised it for me. He made the first step possible. "The step into the situation where faith is possible is not an offer which we can make to Jesus, but always his gracious offer to us."[7]

As a professor in the university, my vocation is limited in its scope, but in my response to the call of Christ my responsibility may be extended. It is difficult in advance to say what is the appropriate restriction or extension of responsibility in my vocation. For example as a professor, I might become involved as a counselor or friend to some student to an extent that was beyond my normal practice or experience. I might offer my opinion on university policy in

---

[7] Bonhoeffer, *Discipleship*, 85.

168

a faculty meeting or I might refrain from it (a time to speak and a time to keep silent). It is impossible to say in advance in these situations what my response might be or should be. Christ calls me to the exercise of free responsibility which is a total response of the whole person to the entirety of reality. "Neither the limitation nor the extension of my responsibility must be based on a principle; the only possible basis for them is the concrete call of Jesus."[8]

One of Bonhoeffer's favorite passages of Scripture when he was in prison is found in the book of the prophet Jeremiah who is speaking to his servant Baruch. "And do you seek great things for yourself? Seek them not, for behold, I am bringing disaster upon all flesh, declares the Lord. But I will give you your life as a prize of war in all places to which you may go."[9] What great work is God calling us into? There is really no way to tell. Maybe there is a small work we can do. It is enough to do the thing that is before us and to take responsible action for the things that are clearly ours. In fulfilling this there is a kind of greater good that emanates throughout our society. We see also in the following quotation that our life in vocation is part of sanctification. The secular work is somehow sanctified and becomes part of our own discipleship.

> But on the basis of their faith and love of neighbor, they are responsible for their own vocation and personal sphere of living, however large or small it is. Wherever this responsibility is faithfully exercised, it has efficacy for the polis as a whole. According to scripture there is no right to

---

[8] Bonhoeffer, *Ethics*, 254.
[9] Jeremiah 45:5.

revolution, but there is a responsibility for all individuals to safeguard the purity of their offices and tasks in the polis. And thus in a genuine sense individuals serve government with their responsibility. No one, [not] even government itself, can take this responsibility from the people or forbid it from being a part of their lives in sanctification, for it derives from obedience to the Lord of the church and of government."[10]

Responsible Business Life

IN HIS BOOK *Ethics*, Dietrich Bonhoeffer makes the following provocative statement, "Jesus took upon Himself the guilt of all men, and for that reason every man who acts responsibly becomes guilty."[11] What exactly does he mean here? First, the desire for some kind of life of perfection must be eschewed. "In all of these [perfectionist] movements we find the attempt to have the Realm of God finally present not only by faith but by sight, no longer veiled within the strange forms of a Christian church, but clearly manifested in the morality and holiness of human beings, and in a perfect solution to all historical and social problems."[12]

A life without error and sin is not possible. Second, selfless love for our neighbor leads to responsible action on

---

[10] Dietrich Bonhoeffer, *Conspiracy and Imprisonment: 1940 – 1945*, DBWE 16 (Minneapolis, MN: Fortress Press, 2006), 525.

[11] Bonhoeffer, *Ethics* 237.

[12] Dietrich Bonhoeffer, *Sanctorum Communio*, DBWE Vol. 1 (Minneapolis, MN: Fortress Press, 1998), 222.

our neighbor's behalf—a willingness to participate in human guilt for the sake of our neighbor.

The world is the place of our responsible action. The world is usually presented in Scripture as a system or a place in opposition to the reign of God. It is the location of sinful action and relationships. However, by fulfilling my vocation as a businessman, I am acting responsibly, but I am not thereby free from guilt or from guilt by association (as if I myself am not a sinner or the persons with whom I associate are not sinners). However, it is not God's will that I cut myself off from this reality. Being in the world can lead us into a more profound understanding of discipleship. For instance, Jesus said to Peter "The one who has bathed does not need to wash, except for his feet, but is completely clean."[13] Dirty feet are evidence of the guilt that I have incurred from my walk in the world—from my responsible action. Christ, evidently, expects the disciples to have dirty feet and he stands ready to wash them on a continual basis. It would be even worse if we tried to maintain clean feet through some kind of overly spiritual refusal to participate in the events at hand. We learn in the Song of Solomon, "I slept, but my heart was awake. A sound! My beloved is knocking 'Open to me, my sister, my love, my dove, my perfect one, for my head is wet with dew, my locks with the drops of the night.' I had put off my garment; how could I put it on? I had bathed my feet; how could I soil them? My beloved put his hand to the latch, and my heart was thrilled within me. I arose to open to my beloved, and my hands dripped with myrrh, my fingers with liquid myrrh, on the

---

[13] John 13:10.

handles of the bolt. I opened to my beloved, but my beloved had turned and gone."[14] The bride here missed a dazzling experience with the bridegroom by refusing to get her feet dirty.

Our walk with Christ is not necessarily an ecstatic rendezvous such as that described in the Song or by St. John of the Cross in *Dark Night of the Soul*, but it is intimately bound up in our vocation and walk in the world. Christ is calling the believer here to get up and to get her feet dirty by seeking Christ in the world, precisely in that place that is opposed to Christ. In this passage in the Song, the woman's failure to eagerly follow Christ into the world resulted in a beating by the watchmen of the city, and rightly so. When did we receive a free pass from the toils and pressures and problematic decisions of the city? Christ did not give us that exemption. Pressures await us; probably sin awaits us in the city. The wise man said "Surely there is not a righteous man on earth who does good and never sins."[15] So we go with a good will as followers of Christ in confidence of His love and continual cleansing as we pursue our vocations.

In responsible business life I understand that I am responsible for other people. For instance, I act on behalf of my children. I am responsible for them. My work also affects my employer, my fellow-workers, the vendors to my company, the ultimate consumer of my company's product. In this I become the businessman for others. Responsibility also means living for others. Responsible living in business does not mean some abject surrender to another, nor setting

---

[14] Song of Solomon 5:2-6.
[15] Ecclesiastes 7:20.

up oneself as some kind of dictator. It does mean surrender to Christ, the ultimate man for others, the ultimate deputy for all of humankind. His action affected the entire human race. Our action in a much smaller way affects others also. Through a Christological perspective the world of things and values finds its proper orientation toward Christ and therefore toward other human beings, since "All things were made through him,..." [16] Therefore, Bonhoeffer states, "Through Christ the world of things and of values is once more directed towards mankind as it was in the Creation." [17]

Responsible business life is not a life of abstract ethics. It is life in the concrete situation, and it is a life of reality. Responsible action does not take its source from ideals but from the knowledge of reality itself. [18] Jesus Christ is the man of reality in whom reconciliation has been accomplished between God and the world. Bonhoeffer mentions that the tragedies of classical antiquity revolve around conflicts between the laws of the gods. These conflicts have been overcome in the person of Christ. Responsible business life becomes a life of simple and confident action within the reconciliation of Christ. Therefore, "The responsible man does not have to impose upon reality a law which is alien to it, but his action is in the true sense in accordance with reality." [19] The Law of God is not some strange code that has been imposed on our world, but it is in harmony with reality because it comes from the heart of reality—Christ himself.

---

[16] John 1:3.
[17] Bonhoeffer, *Ethics*, 223.
[18] Ibid., 226.
[19] Ibid., 224.

"He [Christ] is the real one, the origin, essence and goal of all that is real, and for that reason He is Himself the Lord and the Law of the real. Consequently the word of Jesus Christ is the interpretation of His existence....The words of Jesus are the divine commandment for responsible action..."[20] The words of Scripture are the interpretation of Jesus to us. These words include the Decalogue which is law and is not strange to reality, but on the contrary makes total sense to us. What could be plainer or more applicable than the commandment, "Thou shalt not steal?" This is not an abstract principle but a divine command which can only be applied as we enter the concrete situation. We do not know beforehand how we might apply the commandment. Only the reality and confidence of life in Christ can help us to know that all decision-making should be bounded by love for God and for our neighbor. God and our neighbor form the limit and origin of responsible action.

Bonhoeffer discusses our actions in terms of limited responsibility. We are not trying to put into place an ideological programme of good or some unrestricted principle. Our responsibility is limited by the world in which we live and the concrete situations that disclose themselves to us. We are limited, placed within certain conditions. We are concerned with good will and also the outcome of decisions. We take note of both Kant and Bentham here, and remember that discipleship as Bonhoeffer discusses it, is beyond them but may also use their insights in moral decision-making. We make decisions

---

[20] Ibid., 226.

and take action by observing, weighing-up, assessing and deciding within the limitations of human knowledge in general. "One's task is not to turn the world upside-down, but to do what is necessary at the given place and with a due consideration of reality."[21]

In business there are normal and somewhat predictable courses of events as well as normal consequences of human behavior. To understand these consequences and act accordingly is wisdom. There are techniques of business operation that we do well to master, but then the odd or extraordinary case may confront us. It is these extraordinary cases, possibly cases of necessary action for the survival of the business itself, which appeal to the decision of the actor apart from specific guidelines. Concerning this Bonhoeffer states, "In the economic field it is the destruction of human livelihoods in the interest of the necessities of business."[22] This could be the case of lay-offs or of firing individuals. Again there may be standard practice and procedure concerning this—or perhaps not. We may be confronting an odd case to which decision-making is left to my free responsibility, or even stranger, where I may be forced to decide between my livelihood and the livelihood of another. I may have no decision-making role at all, but simply find myself laid off while doing a good job for the company. There may be no guidelines for employer or employee here.

We don't want to make one of these extraordinary cases into a principle of action. Christ is our principle of action. However, in order to avoid chaos it is necessary to observe

---

[21] Ibid., 230.
[22] Ibid., 235.

law and convention. Observation of standard ways of doing business and business etiquette come to mind here. Law or normal procedure and free responsibility are centers around which our thinking and action in business revolve. Indeed, some people lean more toward one pole and some toward the other. "Each of these men, the one who is bound by the law and the one who acts in free responsibility, must hear and bow before the accusation of the other. Neither can be the judge of the other. It is always for God to judge."[23]

The themes we have emphasized so far are the Law or clear speech of God, free responsibility, and the voluntary acceptance of guilt for the sake of my neighbor. Conscience rebels at this uncertainty, but this abhorrence is based on my attempt to maintain unity with myself. To walk in the law that I have proclaimed or established, i.e. my own knowledge of good and evil, is indeed an attempt to maintain my unity. This shows that I am disunited from my Creator. Indeed, a great change takes place by faith and I find unity again in the person of Jesus Christ, and I become free to accept guilt on behalf of another or make a decision in free responsibility with some uncertainty as to the results. "This means that I can now find unity with myself only in the surrender of my ego to God and to men. The origin and the goal of my conscience is not a law but it is the living God and the living man as he confronts me in Jesus Christ."[24]

Free responsibility is not privilege only for the great, but it is privilege for the worker, the employee, the student, the

[23] Ibid., 236.
[24] Ibid., 240.

apprentice. They must exercise free responsibility side-by-side with obedience. For instance, as I do my duty as professor in terms of preparation, punctuality, timely grading of papers, I also act within a sphere of freedom in my relationships with students, manifested in my encouragement of them or lack thereof. I may choose students in whom I invest more of my time and energy and students with whom I invest less. I can emphasize some aspects of a course and deemphasize others. I must make these decisions freely and entrust the results into the hands of a merciful God. Every job is like this with a larger or a smaller sphere of duty and responsibility and a larger or smaller sphere of free action. "Jesus stands before God as the one who is both obedient and free. As the obedient one He does His Father's will in blind compliance with the law which is commanded Him, and as the free one He acquiesces in God's will out of His own most personal knowledge, with open eyes and a joyous heart;..."[25]

A statement from *The Cost of Discipleship* summarizes responsible business life. "To stay in the world with God means simply to live in the rough and tumble of the world and at the same time remain in the Body of Christ, the visible Church, to take part in its worship and to live the life of discipleship. In so doing we bear testimony to the defeat of this world."[26]

---

[25] Ibid., 248.
[26] Bonhoeffer, *Discipleship*, 260.

Rejection of All Secular New Men

THE AVERAGE PERSON in business is probably not strongly motivated by ideological programs; or are they? Ideology is group think. It is the reification of an idea that succeeds through the force of will or the acquiescence of a large group. It could involve the success of a business through a group of workers who believe an idea and work as if it is already in existence. This kind of ideology is a powerful force. Ideology could be a dream of world peace through the interactions of capitalism. We have seen earlier in Bonhoeffer's "peace speech" at Fanø that he rejected this idea.

Indeed Adam Smith viewed businessmen as creative realists who did not trade much in the realm of ideology or the public good as Smith says here in the famous invisible hand passage. "I have never known much good done by those who affected to trade for the public good. It is an affectation, indeed, not very common among merchants,..."[27] Nevertheless, free market interactions can become a dream and a program subject to ideological manipulation which promises to deliver more than it is able.

With the publication of The Communist Manifesto in 1848, the success of the Bolshevik revolution in Russia, and the rise of National Socialism in Germany, the idea of a "new man" became a theme for philosophy and journalism. This "new man" could be the new Communist man or some kind of Nietzschean superman, or some kind of National

---

[27] Adam Smith, *An Inquiry into the Nature and Causes of the Wealth of Nations* (Chicago: The University of Chicago Press, 1976), 478.

Socialist Teutonic super hero. These ideas and movements were part of Bonhoeffer's time. When ideologues of the "new man" came to power, a definite plan was enacted to produce this new human being. The plan included thought control, propaganda, eugenics, and a hidden world of concentration and prison camps.

To the "new man" of National Socialism might be opposed the "born-again man" of the Christian faith. Indeed we might oppose these totalitarian ideas with the "born-again" person, but what is this person like, or what should she be like? How would this person look in business?

There is no path toward this "born-again" person which proceeds by becoming like famous characters associated with Christ. For example, a person cannot be first like St. Teresa of Avila, then the Virgin Mary and then like Christ. There is no method or programme here. Discipleship in business is differentiated from all ideological and propagandistic efforts. "The content of the Christian message is not that we should become like one of these biblical figures, but that we should be like Christ himself. No method leads to this end, only faith."[28]

So faith produces the "new man"—the "new woman." Bonhoeffer makes this interesting statement in *Ethics*. "The new human beings live in the world like any one else. They often differ very little from other people. They are not concerned to promote themselves, but to lift up Christ for the sake of their brothers and sisters."[29] There is great

---

[28] Dietrich Bonhoeffer, *Ethics*, DBWE vol. 6 (Minneapolis, MN: Fortress Press, 2005), 150.
[29] Bonhoeffer, *Ethics* DBWE, 95.

freedom in being this kind of "new person." We really don't have to believe in an institutional or national dream. The pressures of conformity may cause us to act that way for a time, but as time goes on there stretches out a life of less and less hypocrisy. We perceive less pressure to be "something other, better and more ideal than what one is. God loves the real man. God became a real man."[30]

In his days in prison, Dietrich was content to have lived as the person God intended him to be. There was no remorse for past mistakes. He saw his life as moving within the will of God. "I'm often surprised how little (in contrast to nearly all the others here) I grub among my past mistakes and think how different one thing or another would be today if I had acted differently in the past; it doesn't worry me at all. Everything seems to have taken its natural course, and to be determined necessarily and straightforwardly by a higher providence."[31] The point here is that Bonhoeffer depends on providence (God's guiding hand over our lives in accordance with His purposes), not on some ideological production of the "New Man," whether fascist or communist or new age or capitalist.

The Businessperson as Disciple

IN A SECTION in his book *Ethics*, Bonhoeffer discusses ethical failure by individuals with different personality types.

---

[30] Bonhoeffer, *Ethics* Touchstone, 82.
[31] Dietrich Bonhoeffer, *Letters and Papers from Prison* (New York: Simon & Schuster, 1997), 276.

There are reasonable people, perhaps balanced people, who cannot see either the depths of evil or the depths of the holy. They look for a common-sense "middle way." When the crunch comes they withdraw or yield to the stronger party. We might find the successful corporate-type individual here. Then, there is the ethical fanatic. This is probably a type of person that we don't find in business very often. "The fanatic believes that he can oppose the power of evil with the purity of his will and of his principle." [32] This person eventually tires of the ethical struggle and fades away.

The man with only his conscience as an aid acts solely from this resource. If he has a strong conscience, he is eventually worn down by the whole realm of ethical conflicts that confront him day by day. Strong conscience here means that this individual has no other aid than his own innermost resources.

More at home in business is Bonhoeffer's next type of person—the person of duty. This is a person who fulfills commands, so that responsibility rests with him who gives the command. However, "The man of duty will end by having to fulfill his obligation even to the devil." [33] There is also an entrepreneurial type of person in this discussion. This person acts out of absolute freedom, and "...he values the necessary deed more highly than the spotlessness of his own conscience and reputation..." [34] The actions and consequences for this individual comprise one of the underlying themes of tragedy. Although Bonhoeffer's life

---

[32] Bonhoeffer, *Ethics* Touchstone, 68.
[33] Ibid., 69.
[34] Ibid.

story is certainly more complex than this, here he may have prophesied the final chapters in his own life.

Then there is the person who operates in the realm of private virtuousness. This person keeps the commandments and is more or less oblivious to surrounding evils. This self-imposed ignorance produces further moral consequences. "It is only at the price of self-deception that he can safeguard his private blamelessness against contamination through responsible action in the world. Whatever he may do, that which he omits to do will give him no peace. Either this disquiet will destroy him or he will become the most hypocritical of Pharisees."[35]

This is certainly a discouraging scenario for personal reflection, for we can probably find ourselves in at least one of the preceding types of ethical responses. What is to be done? Bonhoeffer mentions in several of his writings "unreflecting obedience to the will of Christ." Of course, if we reflect on this, obedience loses the quality of spontaneity. Yet we have reflected on several themes from Bonhoeffer's work as they apply to the broad area of life in business. Here is the answer, "All that the follower of Jesus has to do is to make sure that his obedience, following and love are entirely spontaneous and unpremeditated."[36] That may be all one has to do, but to arrive at that point requires a long discipleship journey. In order to avoid an infinite regress of reflection and spontaneity, let's look at some further topics that may help the disciple in business to arrive at unreflective action.

---

[35] Ibid..
[36] Bonhoeffer, *Discipleship*, 159.

We have developed the ideas of the law of God and free responsibility which the disciple in business finds as motivations and limits for action. Exactly how to operate within these two complementarities is difficult, if not impossible, to communicate. In *Ethics*, Bonhoeffer places his own footnote to a sentence in the chapter entitled "The Concrete Commandment and the Divine Mandates." He writes in the body of the text, "Jesus Christ's claim to rule as it is proclaimed by the church simultaneously means that family, culture, and government are set free to be what they are in their own nature as grounded in Christ." [37] He attaches a footnote which states, "Here the antagonism between heteronomy and autonomy is overcome and taken up into a higher unity, which we could call Christonomy." [38] Bonhoeffer finds the answer in the rule or the law of Christ (Christonomy). In other words, I might find these complementary things as two poles between which I swing in terms of decision-making and action. Bonhoeffer finds heteronomy (rule from outside or Divine law) and autonomy (self-rule) taken up into the one Lord Jesus Christ. Sabine Dramm in her book *Dietrich Bonhoeffer: An Introduction to His Thought*, finds the matter this way. "This footnote offers further confirmation that Bonhoeffer's *Ethics* in the final analysis is probably to be understood only dialectically, that is, as a theologically grounded ethics of the autonomy of the believer." [39] The crux of the matter for the

---

[37] Bonhoeffer, *Ethics* DBWE, 402.

[38] Ibid.

[39] Sabine Dramm, *Dietrich Bonhoeffer, an Introduction to His Thought*, tr. By Thomas Rice (Peabody, MA: Hendrickson Publishers, Inc., 2007), 101.

businessperson as disciple seems to be, living in the freedom of Christ (or the Spirit) while taking seriously the law of God. Bonhoeffer had written about this as a much younger man as part of his doctoral work in 1926 in a seminar paper entitled "The Holy Spirit According to Luther."

> Now, Spirit and law are not related in such a way that where the law is the Spirit is as well. This means that the Holy Spirit is not somehow substantially inherent in the law. On the contrary, the Spirit is an active force and blows and operates where it wills. It moves the hearts it wills to move. To be sure, when the law operates, it is moved by the Spirit; and where it is understood, there the divine will moves the human will.[40]

In the same seminar paper Bonhoeffer continues to develop this theme. He talks now of the new person. This is obviously not the "new man" of National Socialism. This is the born-again person acting in freedom. This is not a Christian ideology or a program. This person is living joyously with Christ. His motivation is internal, therefore he lives from himself, and he is creative.

> The law is no longer outside the human person but lies in the new person as a force within. In the same way, the Holy Spirit no longer stands in majesty in opposition to the person, but instead has entered into the person. With this, morality is the law of oneself...i.e., truly spiritual. The spiritual human being, i.e., the truly moral human person, is free from the law and lives from himself, from his spirit.

---

[40] Dietrich Bonhoeffer, *The Young Bonhoeffer*, 1918-1927, DBWE Vol. 9 (Minneapolis: Fortress Press, 2003), 331.

This person creates in spirit in that he acts, and thus is creative.[41]

Bonhoeffer makes similar points in a lecture to his congregation in Barcelona in 1929. The disciple acts in freedom, not under law. She acts according to the spirit of Christ not from principles. Principles here must be conclusions of our ethical reasoning, and as such become iron-clad. Such principles can form a straight-jacket of law as surely as any system of religious law. "...we find the decisive point is that they [some disciples] make the New Testament commandments into new laws and in so doing enslave themselves to those laws, whereas they should be making decisions in freedom. They judge according to the letter rather than according to the spirit of Christ. They act according to principles rather than from the concrete situation of crisis with which God confronts me."[42]

The born-again person is the "new man" and the "new woman" that has been awaited by ideologies of various stripes possibly including a Christian ideology. This born-again person may not exhibit characteristics of victory or rulership, and his life may be largely hidden or unnoticed. These born-again people indeed are all over the world working in many different occupations. Georg Huntemann comments on a famous passage from *The Cost of Discipleship*, "Understood Christ-mystically, being born again means participation in the suffering and death of Christ: '...the cross is not the terrible end to an otherwise god-fearing and happy life, but it meets us at the beginning of our

---

[41] Bonhoeffer, *Young Bonhoeffer*, 345-346.
[42] Bonhoeffer, *Barcelona*, 372.

communion with Christ. When Christ calls a man, he bids him come and die.'"[43] Death with Christ gives confidence and freedom to our actions.

Because of his emphasis on freedom of action, Bonhoeffer's work has been associated with the name of situation ethics which has developed a bad reputation in evangelical circles. Situation ethics is associated with the idea of simply doing what the exigencies of the moment require without regard to principle, command, or prior commitment. This school is associated with the names of Joseph Fletcher the author of *Situation Ethics* and John A. T. Robinson author of *Honest to God*. In fairness, it should be mentioned that Fletcher places Christian decision-making within the context of loving God by loving one's neighbor. Robinson has a chapter in his book entitled "The New Morality," [44] which is similar to Fletcher's work. Both emphasize decision-making in the concrete situation motivated by love alone. Fletcher makes some statements that are contrary to the balance that Bonhoeffer is trying to bring in moral decision-making. For instance Fletcher states, "For the situationist there are no rules—none at all."[45] This must be contrasted with Bonhoeffer's emphasis on the concrete speech of God, particularly as revealed in the Decalogue and the Sermon on the Mount.

---

[43] Georg Huntemann, *Dietrich Bonhoeffer: An Evangelical Reassessment* (Grand Rapids, MI: Baker Books, 1993), 193.

[44] John A.T. Robinson, *Honest to God* (The Westminster Press: Philadelphia, 1963), 105-121.

[45] Joseph Fletcher, *Situation Ethics* (The Westminster Press: Philadelphia, 1966), 55.

The editors of the volume *Conspiracy and Imprisonment*, have added an afterword describing the work on the Freiburg memorandum. This document was written by a group of German theologians who made suggestions for a postwar conference of the World Council of Churches. The impetus for this group was probably provided by the Bishop of Chichester, George Bell, Dietrich's friend. The working group was known as the "Bonhoeffer circle," although he participated in only one meeting in October, 1942. One of the group, Constantin von Dietze took notes of the discussion. "Dietze's notes...are revealing. Key phrases in those notes suggest that there was still fundamental difference of opinion; Bonhoeffer and Perels emphasized their own position of 'Decalogue ethics' over against those, such as Gerhard Ritter, who advocated an 'ethics of conscience.'"[46]

For these reasons, Georg Huntemann states, "Bonhoeffer's ethic is not a situational ethic, but in essence an ethic of responsibility. He was concerned that in each particular, always unique situation the Christian perceives this distinct responsibility to the command of God. Bonhoeffer did not advocate a situational ethics, because his ethic is oriented toward God's command."[47]

---

[46] Bonhoeffer, *Conspiracy*, 662-663.
[47] Huntemann, *Dietrich Bonhoeffer*, 239.

Personal Reflection

WHAT THEN, IS the businessperson as disciple? The answers are multiform and as numerous as the number of Christians in business. Living the Christ-life can appear in many different ways. My own father and mother provide for me a great portrait of Christian discipleship. In fact, their picture hangs in my office with the caption underneath, "Godliness with contentment is great gain."[48] This passage of Scripture is illustrated in their lives.

I had the blessing of God to grow up under the tutelage of a godly Christian father. I see now that Christ was his life. He was a bookkeeper-accountant for a local bank in Jackson, Mississippi. We didn't own a car until I was in the third grade; he walked to work or took the bus.

As I watched him over the years, I began to see that the things he did were some of the things that Christ would do. He fed us. He worked hard. He personally "loaned" (gave) money to people. He took groceries to a crippled newspaper man. He befriended a blind man and took him to church on Sunday. So I began to see that his Christ-life placed him in a certain business context, and Christ lived through my father in various ways for those with eyes to see.

My mother also worked hard at home. The teaching of kindness was on her tongue and she did not eat the bread of idleness. In a certain sense their life together was the normal Christian life. Christ was living through them. At the time I thought this was the way that everyone lived. I see now that they provided me with an unusual example of the Christ life.

---

[48] 1 Timothy 6:6 (KJV).

They indeed entered into the problems of the present time with all the love and energy at their disposal.

"Christians are people of the present in the most profound sense. Be it political and economic problems, moral and religious decline, concern for the present generation of young people—everywhere the point is to enter into the problems of the present, to enter with all the love and all the energy at your disposal."[49] This is how Bonhoeffer had preached to his congregation in Barcelona on the theme of "serving the time," that is, serving God through action appropriate to the times in which we live.

---

[49] Bonhoeffer, *Barcelona*, 529.

CHAPTER 9

AUTHORITY AND POWER

IN THE CONCRETE business situation the young person is encouraged to learn from the older, particularly the mature business person of integrity. I learned my job from my mentor; I also learned responses to different human relationship scenarios while on the job. Theoretical ethical discourse is simply that---theoretical. Business ethics discussions tend to be that way. Even business cases, while useful, lack the earnestness of being personally involved in the case that affects the worker and the company. So, by definition, business ethics discussions must lack the weight of day-to-day business life. There is the lack of a certain ethical authority. Authority relations come to the fore in the midst of concrete cases.

"No one can give themselves authorization for ethical discourse. Rather, it is granted to and bestowed on people, not primarily because of their subjective achievements and distinctions, but because of their objective position in the world." [1] In business ethics there is a recognition of legitimate authority relationships such as boss and employee; master-craftsman and apprentice; supervisor and worker. These authority relationships play an important part in the business ethics universe—that is, in the concrete situation. This is not to negate that all people are formed in *imago dei*, but simply to report the fact that business proceeds under authority.

Authority and power are important themes that are, perhaps, discussed too little in our day. They are most clearly delineated with respect to government and church, but these themes also have relevance for life in business. A person has authority due to occupancy of some position of leadership or direction that is sanctioned, ultimately, by God. Authority connotes an ethical ordering of church or society with a hoped-for, but not necessarily attained, high ethical standard maintained by persons in positions of leadership. It is difficult to discuss a topic like authority because of the extremely democratic tendencies of our age (or perhaps the tendencies of "a world come of age" which desires not to be under the tutelage of any outside party). "This [authority] is an expression of the *orientation from above to below*, which is an intrinsic and essential quality of the ethical, even though it is so highly offensive to the modern mind." [2] However, we come into contact with authority every day, or maybe we see all superior positions as simply power relationships.

---

[1] Dietrich Bonhoeffer, *Ethics* DBWE Vol. 6 (Fortress Press, Minneapolis, MN: 2005), 372.

[2] Bonhoeffer, *Ethics* DBWE, 372.

Authority and Power

Power is the enforcing of directives from a superior by force. In the case of government this is easy to see with the police power being the ultimate sanction for government directives. Business superiors have power through the ability to dismiss from employment or perhaps to withhold promotions, etc. The Church also has power through excommunication or other business-like actions within a Church hierarchy. In business contexts we sometimes hear the phrase, "I have this responsibility, but I don't have the authority to really fulfill it." What is being said is that there is a lack of power to really do the job to which I am assigned. There is an inability to compel others to do certain tasks, or there is an inability to do tasks that are necessary for the adequate fulfillment of responsibility.

In his book *Ethics* and other writings, Dietrich Bonhoeffer treats this topic. The disciple in business should know how to understand and to operate within these realities. Authority derives from God's commandment through the mandates as discussed earlier. There is thus an establishment of above and below with the mandates. The mandates along with corresponding authority roles are not only an historical development, but divine commissions. Those who are in an "above" position might be leaders, government officials, owners of companies, and delegated authorities of all kinds. These authority relationships do not exist simply on the basis of power in which the stronger takes advantage of the weaker. Likewise, authority cannot simply invoke a divine mandate to justify shoddy leadership or bullying tactics. Leadership and followship need each other in a mutually delimiting relationship. Each owes the other respect because of participation in the divine mandate.[3]

Just as lack of belief in a beginning leads to life in the void, so lack of belief in God's mandates leads to abuse of power by leaders and followers, by governors and the governed, by employers and employees. Positions are seen as a matter of fate like the results of a lottery. Occupancy of high position may lead in this case to opportunism and self-centered aggrandizement. A position as one under authority may lead to discontent, outrage, and rebellion. How different is our understanding of authority than that of the Roman centurion who approached Jesus about healing his servant. This centurion had life-and-death authority and power over many legionnaires, but he saw himself primarily as a man under authority. The story is familiar. The centurion says through the mouths of his friends, "For I too am a man set under authority, with soldiers under me: and I say to one, 'Go,' and he goes; and to another, 'Come,' and he comes; and to my servant, 'Do this,' and he does it. When Jesus heard these things, he marveled at him, and turning to the crowd that followed him, said, 'I tell you, not even in Israel have I found such faith'."[4] Jesus links the faith of the centurion to his understanding and practice of authority. The centurion knows who Jesus is because of the mighty works of Jesus and the knowledge that Jesus is under the direct authority of God. Because of the centurion's perception of divine authority, he knows that Jesus can heal

---

[3] Bonhoeffer, *Ethics* DBWE, 390-391.
[4] Luke 7:7-9.

from a distance and does not need to come to the centurion's house

Without the knowledge that "above and below" relationships are established by God within the mandates, abuse of persons can run rampant. Employees can subvert management decisions; they can bring a company down. Managers can abuse workers through manipulation and psychological gamesmanship. The policeman on the beat can treat citizens roughly. Citizens can ignore and despise police authority.

In his incomplete prison novel, Dietrich places these words about authority in the mouth of one of the characters, Major Harald von Bremer, "...it's quite another thing when people exploit the power they have been given over others to humiliate, debase, defile, and destroy them. Then it's no longer a question of tone, it's an outrage, as much against the people concerned as against the office one holds. It desecrates all genuine authority and destroys all human community."[5]

Democratic government has tried to solve the issue of authority through election of officials by the populace. However, this approach also can break down if governmental leaders are seen simply as employees of the people or if the electorate idolizes a leader as some kind of god. The relationship between "above and below" can become warped under such scenarios. "There is no longer an authentic above and below. Instead, those above derive their authorization and legitimation solely from below, and those

---

[5] Dietrich Bonhoeffer, *Fiction from Tegel Prison*, DBWE Vol. 7 (Fortress Press, Minneapolis: 2000), 119.

below regard those who are above—seen from their perspective—merely as the embodied claim of those who are below to get above. Thus those below become an ongoing and inevitable threat to those who are above."[6]

Clear understanding and practice of leadership and followship is a continuing challenge in government, business, and church. In a large organization or group of people, everyone cannot be in leadership. However, businesses and churches cynically offer leadership seminars on a regular basis. One does not often see followship seminars. Perhaps in our "world come of age" this is no longer possible.

Bonhoeffer pondered the problem of authority in the Confessing Church and Protestant churches in general. In a letter to Eberhard Bethge in October, 1940, he writes some thoughts.

> On Sunday we were in Kieckow. We also discussed the church situation. There it became quite clear to me again that the struggle regarding the church government is actually the question necessarily emerging from church history regarding the possibility of a Protestant church for us. It is the question whether, following the separation from papal and worldly authority in the church, an ecclesial authority can be erected that is grounded in word and confession alone. If such an authority is not possible, then the final possibility of a Protestant church is gone; then there truly remains only a return to Rome or a state church or the way into isolation, into the 'protest' of true Protestantism against false authorities. It is no accident but

---

6 Bonhoeffer, *Fiction*, 392.

rather divine necessity that the question today has to do with the authority of true church government.[7]

We have discussed authority and power. Perhaps for the sake of completeness we should mention a third term, spiritual authority. In a certain sense all authority is spiritual since ultimately, it comes from God. However, there is another sense in which authority is spiritual, and this is a matter of discernment. It is possible to discern that a certain disciple has unusual insight into the ways of God or into the word of God. This person might have a kind of "spiritual authority" outside of any office in the church or the world. Happy is the church in which the bishop, the pastor, or the elder bears spiritual authority. In other words, the spiritual authority of the person coincides with the task in the church community. The danger here is the cult of personality. In *Life Together* Bonhoeffer makes the following comment.

> Genuine spiritual authority is to be found only where the service of listening, helping, forbearing, and proclaiming is carried out. Every personality cult that bears the mark of the distinguished qualities, outstanding abilities, powers, and talents of another, even if these are of a thoroughly spiritual nature, is worldly and has no place in the Christian community of faith; indeed, it poisons that community. The longing we so often hear expressed today for 'episcopal figures,' 'priestly people,' 'authoritative personalities' often enough stems from a spiritually sick need to admire human beings and to establish visible human authority because the

---

[7] Dietrich Bonhoeffer, *Conspiracy and Imprisonment: 1940 – 1945*, DBWE Vol. 16 (Minneapolis: Fortress, Press, 2006), 78.

genuine authority of service appears to be too insignificant."[8]

Spiritual authority comes from the Holy Spirit and from maturing discipleship. It is certainly possible for a governmental authority or a businessperson to bear spiritual authority in this sense. That, of course, is not a requirement for the position which is held in government or in business. It is not really a necessary consideration since labor and government operate under their own mandates. As discussed earlier, the mandates of labor, marriage, government and church are given by God and bear their own authority. They support each other and are in tension with each other and thus limit each other.

This mutual limiting safeguards the mandates and safeguards authority. "Being above is thus limited in a threefold way, each of which works differently. It is limited by God who issues the commission, by the other mandates, and by the relation to those below."[9] The relationship between leaders and followers is mutually limiting and confirming. Bad authority relationships can ruin a business organization. Bad attitudes can lower performance and efficiency in the workplace. Understanding and acceptance of authority and authority relationships can lead to mature, healthy relationships between managers and other employees.

For the disciple in business, it is evil passions that must be controlled. Hatred of those above or those below does not

---

[8] Dietrich Bonhoeffer, *Life Together* DBWE Vol. 5 (Minneapolis: Fortress Press, 2005), 106.
[9] Bonhoeffer, *Ethics* DBWE, 394.

belong on the path of discipleship. In his novel from Tegel prison, Bonhoeffer makes this statement concerning abuse of power. The statement comes again from Major von Bremer who is speaking to Franz, the politically left-leaning brother of Christophe who is a figure of Bonhoeffer himself. "...there is in all of us a dark, dangerous drive to abuse the power that is given to us and thereby to destroy life—our own and that of others. Wherever we encounter this truly evil instinct—first of all in ourselves—we must counter it with the force of all the hate and passion we can muster."[10] Our vocations in business provide us with multiple opportunities to put to death these dark, dangerous drives.

---

[10] Bonhoeffer, *Fiction*, 120.

CHAPTER 10

BONHOEFFER'S CONSISTENT ETHICAL RESPONSE:
FROM PACIFIST TO CONSPIRATOR

IN THIS CHAPTER we conclude the meditation on business ethics with a discussion of Dietrich's ethical response to the great ethical issue of his day—namely, the regime of Adolph Hitler. This is not business ethics *per se*, but a look at one man's consistent yet developing ethical understanding and action. This is an extreme case, yet even as persons in business we can be encouraged by his example of continuing theological and ethical reflection. Perhaps in the day of our extreme case, we will not be found wanting.

Bonhoeffer's journey from expounder of pacifism to involvement in the *Abwehr* plot to overthrow Hitler illustrates a consistent ethical response. This may seem to be obviously untrue, but his sister-in-law, Emmi Bonhoeffer and his friend Eberhard Bethge see a consistent ethical and theological development in him. For Emmi Bonhoeffer, "the situations changed and the tasks changed." Bethge sees part of the development in Bonhoeffer's attempt to move from a position of Christian privilege into the concrete situation, from the theoretical to the real. "Bonhoeffer's life consisted of a constant fight to overcome the dangerously privileged character of the Christian religion: in his decision to take up theology, his move from teaching to pastoral work, and then to 'becoming a man for his own times' in the conspiracy against Hitler."[1] Bonhoeffer scholar, Heinz Eduard Tödt states, "Bonhoeffer's theological outline does have a strong continuity in it, from its beginnings to the end. In Bonhoeffer's theology there does exist a stringent connection between Christology, ecclesiology, and ethics."[2]

Bonhoeffer sees his life as following a straight course. Writing from prison to Eberhard Bethge in 1944 he states:

"I heard someone say yesterday that the last years had been completely wasted as far as he was concerned. I'm very glad that I have never yet had that feeling, even for a moment. Nor have I ever regretted my decision in the summer of 1939, for I'm firmly convinced—however strange it may seem—that my life has followed a straight and unbroken course, at any rate in its outward conduct. It has been an uninterrupted enrichment of experience, for which I can only be thankful."[3]

An early development in Bonhoeffer's theology occurred during his year of study at Union Theological Seminary in

[1] Eberhard Bethge, *Dietrich Bonhoeffer: A Biography* (Minneapolis: Fortress Press, 2000), 876.
[2] Heinz Tödt, *Authentic Faith: Bonhoeffer's Theological Ethics in Context* (Grand Rapids: Eerdmans, 2007), 7.
[3] Dietrich Bonhoeffer, *Letters and Papers from Prison* (New York: Simon & Schuster, 1997), 272.

New York. It was his friend Jean Lasserre who pressed the claims of Christ in the Sermon on the Mount toward the conclusion of pacifism. In a letter to Elizabeth Zinn in January, 1936, Dietrich states, "Christian pacifism, which I fought bitterly against...only a short time ago, suddenly became self-evident for me. And this change continued step by step. My views and thoughts revolved around nothing else"[4]

Perhaps we define pacifism too narrowly or force it into a straightjacket in which every kind of coercive action is disavowed. This would not be exactly the model that Christ presents to us with his expulsion of the money-changers from the Temple. As Sabine Dramm states, "Bonhoeffer did not reject every form of force. His oppositional attitude toward the National Socialist system of oppression led him indirectly to participate in plans for a coup. Of necessity, these plans rejected non-violence as a universal principle and consciously accepted force as a means for their implementation. To this extent, his pacifism was relative rather than absolute."[5]

Although pacifism may have been a biblically derived position for Bonhoeffer, it began to be part of his overall opposition to the evil of Nazism and particularly the evil of Adolph Hitler. This opposition successively assumed the forms of pacifism, energetic work in the Confessing Church, Operation Seven [the successful plan to spirit Jews out of Germany into Switzerland], and finally becoming a full-

---

[4] Sabine Dramm, *Dietrich Bonhoeffer: An Introduction to His Thought* (Peabody, MA: Hendrickson Publishers, Inc., 2007), 138.
[5] Dramm, *Dietrich Bonhoeffer*, 139.

fledged member of a conspiracy to kill Hitler which operated within the *Abwehr*. Earlier we saw that Dietrich made a radio broadcast to the nation two days after Hitler's accession to power on January 30, 1933. In the broadcast he warned the listeners of the dangers of a government by some all-powerful leader. His broadcast was cut short, and it is evident that he saw the danger of the whole Hitler phenomenon practically from the start.

At this early date Bonhoeffer's opposition to Hitler was open. His opposition grew during the struggles of the Confessing Church to maintain evangelical doctrine and the freedom to preach, teach, and publish. Later, his beloved Finkenwalde seminarians seemed to pull the most odious duty in the army and they were killed in fighting at an alarming rate. In a note written at the request of von Dohnanyi to the interrogation authorities, Bonhoeffer states, "Over 60% of the Protestant clergy have already been drafted; of those younger clergy belonging to the Confessing Church, over 90%,..." [6] This means that for the young confessing pastors there was no official means of avoiding conscription.

By 1934 Dietrich sensed that the struggle in the Confessing Church was but a portent of things to come. His phrase "resistance to the death," is seen through the lens of the Sermon on the Mount. He writes to Erwin Sutz from London.

And while I'm working with the church opposition with all my might, it's perfectly clear to me that this opposition is

---

[6] Dietrich Bonhoeffer, *Conspiracy and Imprisonment: 1940 – 1945* DBWE 16 (Minneapolis: Fortress Press, 2006), 404.

only a very temporary transitional phase on the way to an opposition of a very different kind, and that very few of those involved in this preliminary skirmish are going to be there for that second struggle. I believe that all of Christendom should be praying with us for the coming of resistance 'to the point of shedding blood' and for the finding of people who can suffer it through. Simply suffering is what it will be about, not parries, blows, or thrusts such as may still be allowed and possible in the preliminary battles, the real struggle that perhaps lies ahead must be one of simply suffering through in faith. Then, perhaps then God will acknowledge his church again with his word, but until then a great deal must be believed, and prayed, and suffered. You know, it is my belief—perhaps it will amaze you—that it is the Sermon on the Mount that has the deciding word on this whole affair.[7]

Eventually, Dietrich's resistance had to become more obscure to his friends, but he continued to express his love for them. Mark Brocker, the editor of the English edition of *Conspiracy and Imprisonment* makes the following comment concerning Bonhoeffer's ministry to his Finkenwalde students through a circular letter to them which is dated August 15, 1941.

Bonhoeffer's letters to the Finkenwalde members, including those who had become soldiers, are eloquent testimony to his continued sense of pastoral ministry to these young men, even as he himself moved into the resistance....contemporary readers will be struck by some phrases in these letters that seem to ignore the reality of what the German army was actually doing. Bonhoeffers's letters of this period to his students, as well his letters to the

---

[7] Dietrich Bonhoeffer, London, 1933-1935, DBWE Vol. 13 (Minneapolis: Fortress Press, 2007), 135.

families of those who had lost someone in the war, should be understood from the perspective of his ministry, his deep affection for former students, and his grief for friends and colleagues who had died in the war. He was naturally also aware that his circular letters were read by Nazi censors. His criticism of the regime, including its atrocities, was expressed through his resistance.[8]

Eberhard Bethge writes of five stages of resistance through which Bonhoeffer and many others passed. The first stage was simple passive resistance such as subverting Gestapo orders not to teach or write. Next came an open resistance to the state on doctrinal and confessional grounds. This stage is characterized by outstanding men such as Martin Niemoeller. The third stage was to become an informed accessory to an impending coup. The fourth stage was participation in preparation for a post-coup government or church organization. The final stage was active involvement in the conspiracy against Adolph Hitler.[9]

Bonhoeffer went through all of these stages. It is interesting to speculate if his increasing involvement in the conspiracy was a result of the National Socialist atrocities against the Jews, or a defense of the gospel through the Confessing Church. The answer is both, yet his defense of the gospel began to take place outside of Confessing Church circles also. His radicalization increased as his disappointment with the Confessing Church increased. The incessant wrangling over the oath of allegiance to Hitler and the silence after the *Kristallnacht* (the night of broken glass)

---

[8] Bonhoeffer, *Conspiracy*, 207.
[9] Eberhard Bethge, *Dietrich Bonhoeffer: A Biography*, (Minneapolis: Fortress Press, 2000), 792.

pogrom of November 9, 1938 caused Dietrich to distance himself from the Church.

Sabine Dramm argues that by 1941 Bonhoeffer was firmly involved in the conspiracy because of his resistance to atrocities against the Jews.

> By this time—we need only remember the deportation reports from the autumn of 1941—Bonhoeffer had irrevocably crossed the threshold into a double existence of subversion. A thorough study of his attitude toward the Jews shows that "it was the escalation of discrimination against the Jews that prompted Bonhoeffer to escalate his own opposition toward the NS-State into active resistance." It was at this time that he deliberately assisted others, such as Charlotte Friedenthal, in fleeing, thus participating in the activity that has gone into the history books as Operation Seven.[10]

The course of one's life is influenced and determined by the surrounding circumstances, both major events and minor. In Bonhoeffer's case a report to the state police pushed him in the direction of increasing radicalization. A report was given to the police that Pastor Bonhoeffer was leading a small Bible-study retreat in the little village of Blöstau. There were only a handful of students in attendance, however, the police banned Dietrich from public speaking throughout the Reich as a result of this. He was thereafter required to report his movements to the police at Schlawe, his official place of residence. This event narrowed his options and caused him to align even more closely with the military intelligence

---

[10] Dramm, *Dietrich Bonhoeffer*, 170.

group.[11] The point is that he was resisting Hitler from the very beginning. The question was, "How to resist most effectively and what options do I have?"

In Dietrich's opposition to the Hitler regime, he did not simply ignore the theological and ethical themes that he had developed over his lifetime. Beginning with early lectures at the University of Berlin in *Creation and Fall*, he characterizes forgetting God's law as a trick of the devil. There is a kind of overplaying of the theme of God's grace so that we can forgive ourselves as we are planning to sin.[12] Bonhoeffer never fell for this illusion as evidenced when he expounded the passage from Matthew 26:52, "all who take the sword will perish by the sword," at the request of Hans von Dohnanyi and the *Abwehr* group of conspirators. He told them frankly that the judgment of God would fall on them as well, so that each one would have to take responsibility for his own actions.[13]

In his book *Prayerbook of the Bible: An Introduction to the Psalms*, written at the height of Nazi opposition to any honoring of the Old Testament, Dietrich teaches the meaning of the imprecatory psalms. This little book is a result also of his love of praying through the Psalms. However, there is a stern anti-Nazi stance declared here simply by the writing and publishing of this book at this particular time. "Nowhere do those who pray these [imprecatory] psalms want to take revenge into their own

[11] Bonhoeffer, *Conspiracy and Imprisonment*, 648.
[12] Dietrich Bonhoeffer, *Creation and Fall: Temptation* (New York: Macmillan Publishing Company, 1953), 123.
[13] Eberhard Bethge, *Dietrich Bonhoeffer: A Biography* (Minneapolis: Fortress Press, 2000), 625.

hands; they leave vengeance to God alone. Therefore they must abandon all personal thoughts of revenge and must be free from their own thirst for revenge; otherwise vengeance is not seriously left to God."[14] Conspiracy in the plot to overthrow Hitler was not a case of revenge, clearly. For Bonhoeffer, it was defense of the flock.

Pastor Bonhoeffer

DIETRICH BONHOEFFER was a pastor. He was a pastor to a group of young people in the working-class district of Wedding in Berlin. He was pastor to a group of young seminarians at Zingst and Finkenwalde. He was pastor to congregations in Barcelona and London. He was pastor to larger groups within the Confessing Church by fighting fiercely against any Nazification of doctrine particularly with respect to ignoring the Old Testament. He was shepherding the flock in the finest patristic tradition where theology was seen as always pastoral theology. The sheep must be protected by defending the faith at the points where it is being attacked. Dietrich was passionately involved in this through his defense of the Barmen and Dahlem declarations, and his courageous words of encouragement to his fellow pastors to defend the faith against the encroachments of Nazism.

---

[14] Dietrich Bonhoeffer, *Prayerbook of the Bible* DBWE Vol. 5 (Minneapolis: Fortress Press, 2005), 174-175.

These efforts eventually failed and Dietrich found himself more and more marginalized. His last defense of the faith was in the conspiracy against Adolph Hitler. Bonhoeffer would not recommend that anyone necessarily follow him in this. This was his last attempt to resist evil and to defend the faith.

To place his story in a more modern context, let's say that you are the pastor of a local congregation. You are the shepherd of the flock. Let's say a mentally deranged person enters the church and begins to beat a widow who is seated on the back pew of the church. What is your responsibility? You must interpose yourself between the widow and the madman and attempt to subdue him. If the level of physical violence escalates, you must do your duty as a representative of Christ and shepherd of the flock. In that sense, Bonhoeffer was a pastor to the German people and he was doing his duty to subdue the madman. Indeed, in his famous phrase from *Letters and Papers from Prison*, he was becoming the man for others.

In the dark days of 1941, some correspondence from Willem Visser't Hooft, the secretary of the provisional World Council (predecessor of the World Council of Churches) is illuminating. Visser't Hooft lived in Geneva, Switzerland from which he had also been secretary of the Life and Work section of the old World Alliance. In 1938 he and Bonhoeffer had an extended conversation concerning the impending war. Bonhoeffer raised question after question about the effects of a war on the Confessing Church in Germany. Visser't Hooft remembered the questions better than the answers. Clearly, they were both exploring the ethical path, the path of action that the churches should take.

Dietrich had previously written a position paper entitled "State and Church," in which he outlined causes for church non-compliance with directives from the state.

> The duty of Christians to obey binds them up to the point where the government forces them into direct violation of the divine commandment, thus until government overtly acts contrary to its divine task and thereby forfeits its divine claim. When in doubt, obedience is demanded,...But if government oversteps its task at some point—e.g., by making itself lord over the faith of the church-community—then at this point it is indeed to be disobeyed for the sake of conscience and for the sake of the Lord. [15]

Visser't Hooft's "Notes on the State of the Church in Europe," mentions a leaked Nazi document which gave a clear idea of the course of policy toward the Church. This policy included, "vigorous control of Church finance by the State; no religious instruction except in the church-building; the dissolution of church movements among youth; no membership of the church except by definite declaration and not under 21 years of age; no contact of regional churches with each other." [16] This policy was obviously designed to further marginalize the church, to give it no place in national life or culture. In a document written by Bonhoeffer and Friedrich Justus Perels entitled "Petition to the Armed Forces," it is clear that the state was moving into a more fierce opposition to the Church.

---

[15] Bonhoeffer, *Conspiracy,* 516-517.
[16] Ibid., 176.

The Gestapo's treatment of pastors at interrogations, etc., is now in general the same as that of criminals....The killing of so-called unworthy lives, which has now become better known in the congregations and has claimed its victims from them, is viewed by Christians of all confessions with the deepest alarm and with revulsion, especially in connection with the general abrogation of the Ten Commandments and any security of law and thus as a sign of the anti-Christian stance of leading authorities in the Reich.[17]

The point here is that the Nazi state was moving into a more apocalyptic, anti-Christ stance. The apocalyptic state is the state of the end time. Even in the midst of persecutions of the church, Bonhoeffer didn't believe that the Third Reich was necessarily heralding the immediate coming of Christ. There is an authentic and an inauthentic apocalypticism. "The being of government is connected with a divine task.... A complete apostasy from its task would call its being into question. However, by God's providence this complete apostasy is only possible as an eschatological event. There, under severe martyrdom, it leads to the church-community's complete separation from the government as the embodiment of the anti-Christ."[18]

At a meeting in Switzerland, Willem Visser't Hooft had asked Dietrich about the direction of his prayers in the present situation. Bonhoeffer responded, "If you want to know, I pray for the defeat of my country, for I think that is the only possibility of paying for all the suffering that my

---

[17] Ibid., 244-245.
[18] Ibid., 514.

country has caused the world."[19] Other Christians and high church officials were praying for the same thing. Dietrich met with other ecumenical leaders in Sigtuna, Sweden in May, 1942 where plans for a coup against Hitler were discussed with the approbation of these ecumenical leaders. It seems unpatriotic, however, if one turns on the leader of one's own country. The prophet Jeremiah was in a similar position of being unpatriotic when he counseled submission to the invading King of Babylon rather than fighting against him.

Even in such dark days, Dietrich tried to maintain happiness in the penultimate things that surround us—the good things of life that give us joy. In wedding congratulations to Gustav Seydel of 1942 he comments, "What always delights me in news like this is the self-assured glimpse into the future and the confidence that there is a reason to look forward to the next day or the next year, the joyful grasping hold of happiness where God still gives it to us. This is—don't misunderstand me—a protest against all false, inauthentic apocalypticism that is becoming so widespread today, and I hail it as a sign of authentic and healthy faith."[20]

The Borderline Case

BONHOEFFER'S INVOLVEMENT in the conspiracy to assassinate Hitler was a result of reflection, previous actions,

---

[19] Bethge, 744.
[20] Bonhoeffer, *Conspiracy*, 328.

and the varying circumstances and choices of life. His involvement occurred at an unusual and horrific time in history. This would not be "normal" ethical action, therefore, we move into a discussion of the "borderline case" or the "boundary situation." Bonhoeffer discussed the borderline case in several texts. In *Ethics* it is discussed as the last resort or the borderline case in which the stakes are very high and normal reasoning has run out of alternatives. This case, says Bonhoeffer, moves into the area of the irrational, and for that reason the borderline case cannot be made into a rule, a norm, or a technique.[21]

In his essay "After Ten Years," which was written as a Christmas gift for General Oster and Hans von Dohnanyi, he states that historically important action oversteps the limits of law.

"But it makes all the difference whether such overstepping of the appointed limits is regarded in principle as the superseding of them, and is therefore given out to be a law of a special kind, or whether the overstepping is deliberately regarded as a fault which is perhaps unavoidable, justified only if the law and the limit are re-established and respected as soon as possible."[22] Indeed, it does make all the difference. Bonhoeffer's interpreters see his action in both of these ways—some as a borderline case, some as a norm. Dietrich, of course, pondered this conundrum. "At first I wondered a good deal whether it was really for the cause of Christ that I was causing you all such grief; but I soon put

---

[21] Dietrich Bonhoeffer, *Ethics* DBWE Vol. 6 (Minneapolis: Fortress Press, 2005), 273.

[22] Dietrich Bonhoeffer, *Letters and Papers from Prison* (New York: Simon & Schuster, 1997), 10-11.

that out of my head as a temptation, as I became certain that the duty had been laid on me to hold out in this boundary situation with all its problems; I became quite content to do this, and have remained so ever since (1 Peter 2.20; 3.14)."[23]

Joachim von Soosten in the editor's afterword to the German edition of *Sanctorum Communio* uses the phrase "vicarious representative action" to describe Bonhoeffer's journey toward the resistance against Hitler. "The church exists for others," and "The man for others," were typical phrases of Bonhoeffer's theology. The disciple of Christ acts as a representative for Christ in action toward others. In prison this line of thought became more identified with a radical theology of the cross, i.e. vicariously representing Christ's suffering on the cross. As Dietrich stated, "It is the most radical expression of the idea that God's truth, although already real, can and even must become true only in the reality of the world through the witness of persons who in vicarious representative action mutually stand-up-for-each-other. Only thus can this truth be expressed 'nonreligiously.'"[24]

Bonhoeffer's famous "non-religious interpretation" of Christianity centers around Christology—the study of Christ, "the man for others." This is essentially living out the Christ life. Eberhard Bethge makes this comment concerning this borderline case.

With this theology of his final months Bonhoeffer—consciously or unconsciously—prevented his career of

---

[23] Bonhoeffer, *Letters*, 129.
[24] Dietrich Bonhoeffer, *Sanctorum Communio* DBWE Vol. 1 (Minneapolis: Fortress Press, 1998), 304.

solidarity (with the members of the political resistance), which began as a 'borderline case,' from remaining such; he thereby prevented an easy dismissal of this solidarity. Suddenly this 'borderline case' is made visible and validly interpreted as an example of being Christian today, both in its task and in its destiny. This theology and this life were a breakthrough, in which the nature of this exceptional path revealed itself as the future normality: 'being for others' as sharing in the suffering of Jesus.[25]

To this Sabine Dramm opposes, "...the borderline situation and its guilt remained for him [Bonhoeffer] a unique exception, precisely as his own decision to collaborate in conspiracy, and the guilt it involved, was and remained for him likewise a borderline case, a unique exception."[26]

Is Bonhoeffer's conspiratorial involvement a unique exception or the future normality? The times and circumstances were exceptional. Bonhoeffer's involvement as a highly educated and thoughtful theologian were exceptional, but Bethge's use of the term "future normality" is hopeful. If disciples see Jesus as "the man for others", and in imitation of Him begin to be men and women for others, what an outflowing of Christian proclamation and goodwill could result.

Dietrich's involvement was for the good of others. In its waning days the National Socialist state had called for a day of "National Sacrifice." This was simply a collection of goods which might be used by others in the populace. His last letter from prison was written to his parents on January 17, 1945.

---

[25] Bethge, 886.
[26] Dramm, 181.

Dear Parents,

I'm writing to you today because of the 'National Sacrifice,' and want to ask you to feel entirely free to dispose of my belongings....

The past two years have taught me how little one can make do with.

The inactivity of long imprisonment is an especially strong incentive to do everything possible, within one's limited power, for the common good.[27]

The good of others, the common good—these were themes that motivated Dietrich until the end. These were the overriding factors in the conspiracy against Hitler.

---

[27] Bonhoeffer, *Letters*, 272.

EPILOGUE:

CHRISTIAN FORMATION IN THE BUSINESS SCHOOL

IN 1999, JAMES COWAN made a pilgrimage to Mount Colzim in Egypt, the abode of Saint Anthony of the desert in the second century. From here he made other journeys to centers of ancient monastic life. He brings a report from Abdishó Hazzaya, a famous ascetic who died around 690 in Maragna Monastery in Central Iraq between the Tigris and Euphrates rivers. Abdishó gives five signs or stages through which the ascetic must pass to attain the highest state of serenity. "According to Abdishó, the first sign is determined by a renunciation of the world brought about by a love of solitude."[1] It is here that we encounter a different approach to knowing Christ, the mystical approach. However, many of us do not have that love of solitude and are meant to live

---

[1] James Cowan, *Desert Father, A Journey in the Wilderness with Saint Anthony* (Boston: Shambhala, 2004), 140.

in marriage—in community. "It is not good that the man should be alone."[2] Our married life or community life causes us to be in regular interaction with people. It causes us to be in interaction with the world—in this case, the world of business.

There must be a way that Christ will reveal Himself to us here—and there is. We have discussed the way of wisdom given to us particularly in Proverbs. This way leads through the rough and tumble of human interaction in all its forms. In terms of finding the knowledge of God, evidently there is an internal, meditative way to seek the wisdom of God who is Christ in us. However, the Book of Proverbs is a book of advice concerning practical action in the world. So, this path of practical action may also lead to a contemplation of Christ and a love for God. It seems that we are continuing an ancient discussion of the active life versus the contemplative life, and perhaps we are. However, the path of practical action in the business world may lead to the knowledge of God that we are discussing. This knowledge is found in the midst of the action and ethical decision that surround us. Bonhoeffer states in *The Cost of Discipleship*, "The otherworldliness of the Christian life ought, Luther concluded, to be manifested in the very midst of the world, in the Christian community and in its daily life."[3] "To stay in the world with God means simply to live in the rough and tumble of the world and at the same time remain in the Body of Christ."[4]

---

[2] Genesis 2:18.
[3] Dietrich Bonhoeffer, *The Cost of Discipleship* (New York: Simon & Schuster, 1995), 265.
[4] Bonhoeffer, *Discipleship*, 260.

Christian Formation in the Business School

In a letter from prison, Dietrich discusses Eberhard Bethge's distaste for a total interest or delight in commercial concerns. "In the end, however, the one who is really intact as a person always has the greater authority."[5] Perhaps he means here spiritual authority or wholeness or shalom. "...the Bible does not recognize our distinction between the outward and the inward. Why should it? It is always concerned with *anthropos teleios*, the *whole* man, ...The 'heart' in the biblical sense is not the inner life, but the whole man in relation to God."[6]

In Christian schools of business, this is the type of student that we are interested in encouraging—a student with some wholeness, some balance, some conscious pursuit of Christ.

In the schools of business in Christian universities we do occasionally endure a lecture by a successful businessperson who not only delights in commerce, but evidently delights *only* in commerce. Our vocations lead us into business, into commerce. To enjoy our vocation is good as Scripture teaches. However, to delight *only* in commerce is but a short step to delighting in greed. But to glory in greed is, as the Apostle says, "to glory in our shame." We tolerate this, and in effect say that greed is good. This is our great error, and one that we must eradicate.

To be successful in business is one thing. To have the gift of making money, even lots of it, is just that—a gift. This success is, however, a means to an end or maybe several

---

[5] Dietrich Bonhoeffer, *Letters and Papers from Prison* (New York: Simon & Schuster, 1997), 238.
[6] Bonhoeffer, *Discipleship*, 346.

ends—our own sustenance, provision of employment for others, a path of activity in which the life of Christ can be lived, the means by which God provides for our needs. Success in business, however, is not meant (by God) to be a platform for nourishing greed.

Greed is sin. It is sin against which I pray. It is sin against which my father (a smart stock investor) prayed. We must teach these things in the business school. We must teach the difference between earning money and greed. They are not the same thing. Wisdom and spiritual authority can also be learned and gained in the world of business and commerce. This is the path to which we need to direct our students. We can then discern the difference between business people who are merely successful and those who have authority.

How can Christian schools of business teach students in a way that is different from the purely secular approach? Perhaps we should concentrate more on living the Christ-life with our business students. For example, in business ethics classes in addition to the standard ethics material and case work, perhaps some attempt at spiritual formation should be made.

I have in mind an addition to business ethics that would require students to keep a daily journal with respect to some particular teaching from Proverbs. The assignment will be to select a specific text and attempt to live out that text for one day, and then to report the results in a journal. This, of course, is one idea. There are several good books on discipleship that could be read, discussed, and practiced as part of the assigned coursework. This can be done at

Christian schools because they are, precisely, Christian schools. Spiritual formation is too important to be left to departments of theology or Bible. In leaving spiritual formation to the Bible departments, this has had a tendency to further ghettoize the Christian life—to leave it in the church building, or to leave it to the experts while we engage in our normal secular life. This is not the model of Christian discipleship that we want to present. Perhaps, by God's grace, we can do better.

REFERENCES

Ancient Christian Commentary on Scripture. Vol. IX. Downers Grove, IL: InterVarsity Press, 2005.

Augustine. *The City of God.* New York: The Modern Library, 1950.

Bentham, Jeremy. *An Introduction to the Principles of Morals and Legislation.* Edited by W. Harrison. Oxford: The Clarendon Press, 1948.

Bethge, Eberhard, *Dietrich Bonhoeffer: A Biography.* Edited by Victoria J. Barnett. Translated By Eric Mosbacher, Peter and Betty Ross, Frank Clarke, and William Glen-Doepel under Editorship of Edwin Robertson. Minneapolis: Fortress Press, 2000.

Bethge, Eberhard, Renate Bethge, and Christian Gremmels, *Dietrich Bonhoeffer: A Life in Pictures.* Translated by John Bowden. London: SCM Press, 1986.

von Bismarck, Ruth-Alice, and Ulrich Kabitz. *Love Letters from Cell 92.* Nashville, TN: Abingdon Press, 1995.

DBWE stands for Dietrich Bonhoeffer Works, English edition, translated from *Dietrich Bonhoeffer Werke* the definitive edition of Bonhoeffer's writings published in Germany by Chr. Kaiser Verlag and edited by Eberhard Bethge. The translation project of these works into English is occurring under the auspices of the International Bonhoeffer Society. Wayne Whitson Floyd Jr., General Editor. Minneapolis: Fortress Press, 1996-.

Bonhoeffer, Dietrich. *Sanctorum Communio.* DBWE Vol. 1. Edited by Clifford Green. Translated by Reinhard Krauss and Nancy Lukens. Minneapolis: Fortress Press, 1998.

———. *Act and Being.* DBWE Vol. 2. Edited by Wayne Whitson Floyd, Jr. Translated by H. Martin Rumscheidt. Minneapolis: Fortress Press, 1996.

———. *Life Together: Prayerbook of the Bible, An Introduction to the Psalms.* DBWE Vol. 5. Edited by Geffrey B. Kelly. Translated by Daniel W. Bloesch and James H. Burtness. Minneapolis: Fortress Press, 2005.

———. *Ethics.* DBWE Vol. 6. Edited by Clifford J. Green. Translated by Reinhard Krauss, Charles C. West, and Douglas W. Stott. Minneapolis: Fortress Press, 2005.

———. *Fiction from Tegel Prison.* DBWE Vol. 7. Edited by Clifford J. Green. Translated by Nancy Lukens. Minneapolis: Fortress Press, 2000.

———. *The Young Bonhoeffer, 1918-1927.* DBWE Vol. 9. Edited by Paul Duane Matheny, Clifford J. Green and Marshall D. Johnson. Translated by Mary C. Nebelsick and Douglas W. Stott. Minneapolis: Fortress Press, 2003.

———. *Barcelona, Berlin, New York, 1928-1931.* DBWE Vol. 10. Edited by Clifford J. Green. Translated by Douglas W. Stott. Minneapolis: Fortress Press, 2008.

———. *London, 1933-1935.* DBWE Vol. 13. Edited by Keith Clements. Translated by Isabel Best. Minneapolis: Fortress Press, 2007.

_____. *Conspiracy and Imprisonment, 1940-1945*. DBWE Vol. 16. Edited by Mark S. Brocker. Translated by Lisa E. Dahill, supplementary material by Douglas W. Stott. Minneapolis: Fortress Press, 2006.

_____. *The Cost of Discipleship*. Translated by R.H. Fuller. New York: Simon & Schuster, 1995.

_____. *Creation and Fall, Temptation*. Translated by John C. Fletcher. New York: Macmillan Publishing Company, 1959.

_____. *Ethics*. Translated by Neville Horton Smith. New York: Simon & Schuster, 1995.

_____. *Letters and Papers from Prison*. Translated by Reginald Fuller and Frank Clark. New York: Simon & Schuster, 1997.

Coppleston, Frederick. *Modern Philosophy: A History of Philosophy*. Volume VII. New York: Image Books, 1994.

Cowan, James. *Desert Father, A Journey in the Wilderness with Saint Anthony*. Boston: Shambhala Publications, Inc., 2004.

Dietrich Bonhoeffer: Memories and Perspectives, Trinity Films, 1983.

Dramm, Sabine. *Dietrich Bonhoeffer, An Introduction to His Thought*. Translated by Thomas Rice. Peabody, MA: Hendrickson Publishers Inc., 2007.

Fauna and Flora of the Bible. 2nd edition. New York: United Bible Societies, 1980.

Fletcher, Joseph. *Situation Ethics*. Philadelphia: The Westminster Press, 1966.

Harris, R. Laird, Gleason Archer, and Bruce Waltke. *Theological Wordbook of the Old Testament*. Vol. I. Chicago: Moody Press, 1980.

Huntemann, Georg. *Dietrich Bonhoeffer: An Evangelical Reassessment*. Translated by Todd Huizinga. Grand Rapids, MI: Baker Book House, 1996.

Hutcheson, Francis. *A Short Introduction to Moral Philosophy*. Hildesheim: George Oms Verlagsbuchhandlung. 1971.

Kreeft, Peter J. *The Philosophy of Tolkien*. San Francisco: Ignatius Press, 2005.

Letwin, Shirley R. *The Pursuit of Certainty*. Indianapolis: Liberty Fund, 1998.

Lopez, José, and José Santos. "Smithian Perspective on the Markets of Beliefs." *Journal of Markets and Morality*. 11 (1) Spring, 2008.

Lightfoot, J.B. *The Apostolic Fathers*. Grand Rapids, MI: Baker Book House, 1978.

McCloskey, Deirdre. *The Bourgeois Virtues*. Chicago: University of Chicago Press, 2006.

Miller, Arthur. *Death of a Salesman*. Edited by Gerald Weales. New York: The Viking Press, 1968.

Moberg, D.J. "Practical Wisdom and Business Ethics," *Business Ethics Quarterly.*, 17 (3) 2007.

Niebuhr, H. Richard. *Christ and Culture*. New York: Harper Torchbooks, 1975.

Neibuhr, Reinhold. "To America and Back," *I Knew Dietrich Bonhoeffer*, Edited by Wolf-Dieter Zimmerman. New York: Harper & Row, 1966.

Nelson, F. Burton. "The Life of Dietrich Bonhoeffer," *The Cambridge Companion to Dietrich Bonhoeffer*. Edited by John de Gruchy. Cambridge: Cambridge University Press, 2002.

The Reformation Study Bible, English Standard Version, Edited by R.C. Sproul, Orlando, FL: Ligonier Ministries, 2005.

Robinson, John A.T. *Honest to God*. Philadelphia: The Westminster Press, 1963.

Rumscheidt, Martin. "The Formation of Bonhoeffer's Theology," *The Cambridge Companion to Dietrich Bonhoeffer*. Edited by John de Gruchy. Cambridge: Cambridge University Press, 2002.

Shaw, William, and Vincent Barry. *Moral Issues in Business*. 10th ed., Belmont, CA: Thomson Wadsworth, 2007.

Smith, Adam. *An Inquiry into the Nature and Causes of the Wealth of Nations*. Edited by Edwin Canaan. Chicago: The University of Chicago Press, 1976.

Smith's Dictionary of the Bible. Vol. II, Edited by H.B. Hackett. Boston: Houghton, Mifflin and Company, 1889.

Sullivan, Roger J. *An Introduction to Kant's Ethics*. New York: Cambridge University Press, 1997.

Tödt, Heinz. *Authentic Faith: Bonhoeffer's Theological Ethics in context*. Edited by Ernst-Albert Scharffenorth and Glen Harold Stassen. Translated by David Stassen and Ilse Tödt. Grand Rapids: Eerdmans, 2007.

Velasquez, Manuel G. *Business Ethics*, 4th ed. Upper Saddle River, New Jersey: Prentice Hall, 1998.

Wilkin, Robert. *The Church's Bible: The Song of Songs*. Grand Rapids, MI: William B. Eerdmans Company, 2003.

Wind, Renate, *Dietrich Bonhoeffer; A spoke in the Wheel*. Grand Rapids, Michigan: Wm. B. Eerdmans, 1998.

Zimmerman, Wolf-Dieter. "Years in Berlin," *I Knew Dietrich Bonhoeffer*. Edited by Wolf-Dieter Zimmerman. New York: Harper & Row, 1966.

ACKNOWLEDGEMENTS

Reprinted with the permission of Scribner, a Division of Simon & Schuster, Inc., from THE COST OF DISCIPLESHIP by Dietrich Bonhoeffer, translated from the German by R.H. Fuller, with revisions by Irmgard Booth. Copyright © 1959 by SCM Press Ltd. All rights reserved.

Reprinted with the permission of Scribner, a Division of Simon & Schuster, Inc., from LETTERS AND PAPERS FROM PRISON, REVISED by Dietrich Bonhoeffer, translated from the German by R.H. Fuller, Frank Clark, et al. Copyright © 1953, 1967, 1971 by SCM Press Ltd. All rights reserved.

Reprinted with the permission of Scribner, a Division of Simon & Schuster, Inc., from ETHICS by Dietrich Bonhoeffer, translated from the German by Neville Horton. Copyright © 1955 by SCM Press Ltd. Copyright © 1955 by Macmillan Publishing Company. All rights reserved.

Reprinted with the permission of Scribner, a Division of Simon & Schuster, Inc., from CREATION AND FALL: A THEOLOGICAL EXPOSITION OF GENESIS 1-3 by Dietrich Bonhoeffer, edited by Martin Ruter and Ilse Todt, and translated from the German Edition by Douglas Stephen Bax. Copyright © 1997 by SCM Press Ltd. And Macmillan Publishing Company. All rights reserved.

"Death of a Salesman", from ARTHUR MILLER'S COLLECTED PLAYS by Arthur Miller, copyright © 1957 by Arthur Miller. Used by permission of Viking Penguin, a division of Penguin Group (USA) Inc.

Reprinted by permission of HarperCollins Publishers, from ACT AND BEING by Dietrich Bonhoeffer and translated by Bernard Noble. Copyright © 1956 by Christian Kaiser Verlag. Translation copyright © 1961 by William Collins & Sons, Ltd. And Harper & Brothers Inc.

Reprinted by permission of HarperCollins Publishers, from THE COMMUNION OF SAINTS by Dietrich Bonhoeffer. Copyright © 1960 by Christian Kaiser Verlag. Copyright © 1963 in the English translation by William Collins & Co. Ltd., London, and Harper & Row, Inc., New York. Copyright renewed 1991.

Reprinted by permission of HarperCollins Publishers, from LIFE TOGETHER by Dietrich Bonhoeffer and translated by John Doberstein. English translation copyright © 1954 by Harper & Brothers, copyright renewed 1982 by Helen S. Doberstein.

From SHAW/BARRY. *Moral Issues in Business*, 11E. © 2010 Wadsworth, a part of Cengage Learning, Inc. Reproduced by permission. www.cengage.com/permissions

Reprinted with the permission of Augsburg Fortress Publishers / Augsburg Fortress, see Fortress Press volumes in Bibliography.

About the Author

WALTON PADELFORD received his Ph.D. in economics from Louisiana State University in 1975 and has taught economics and business ethics at Union University in Jackson, Tennessee since 1980.

He has published several peer-reviewed journal articles and scholarly articles in the field of business ethics and is currently University Professor of Economics at Union.

CPSIA information can be obtained at www.ICGtesting.com
Printed in the USA
LVOW061511280313

326538LV00021B/1252/P